THE SOUL
OF A BOY

The Soul of a Boy: True-life tales full of the wit and warmth of childhood
Copyright © 2016-18 by Troy Kidder. All rights reserved.
PureBlueCreative.com

No part of this publication may be reproduced, stored in a retrieval system or transmitted in any way by any means, electronic, mechanical, photocopy, recording or otherwise without the prior permission of the author except as provided by USA copyright law.

Book cover and interior design by Russell Lake - SeedStudios.com

ISBN: 978-1-7328712-0-5 (Paperback)
ISBN: 978-1-7328712-1-2 (Hard Cover)
ISBN: 978-1-7328712-2-9 (Electronic Edition)

Library of Congress Number: 2018911842

1. Self-Help / Motivational & Inspirational
2. Humor / Form / Jokes & Riddles
16.01.15 - 18.10.01

PRINTED IN THE UNITED STATES OF AMERICA

THE SOUL
OF A BOY

True-life tales
full of the wit
and warmth
of childhood

TROY KIDDER

PREFACE

These stories are from the heart. Since I often write late at night and sometimes into the wee hours of the morning, even my family does not always witness the process. But I've been known to laugh uncontrollably and even sob like a baby while writing these stories. They are that real and intimate to me.

It's funny. The number one question I am always asked is "Are these stories really true?" Yes, as odd and quirky as they appear, I lived these tales. While most of my stories are one hundred percent accurate, the percentage of accuracy for some may drop a bit by the natural process of time or just plain writer's license. I doubt that you will discern which parts may have been added for dramatic purposes. I doubt that, since I'm not sure I could either.

One thing's for sure. What you are about to read certainly proves the old adage "Truth is stranger than fiction." It is my hope that as you go on these little adventures, you will discover the truth—that life is to be enjoyed, that every life matters and that we truly need each other.

Troy

TABLE OF CONTENTS

THE EARLY YEARS
First Day of School and a Furry
   Bathroom Rug 1
The Kiss of Spring 4
The Harley Hogs of Amish Country .. 7
Sweet Potato Pants 10
The Cow Patty Cruiser 13
Oh, Say Can You See–or at
   Least Play Guitar 17
I Long to Live in a
   Neighborhood Again 20
Rise to the Occasion 24
A Boy and His Rex 27
Big Boots, Big Heart 31
The Sole of a Shoe and the
   Soul of a Boy 35
The Song of Summer 39
Drifting Like Snow 42
Back to the Tree Trunk 45
A Shot at History 49
The 'Mark' of our Neighborhood 53
The Spank 56
Pretend Pups for Sale 60
Trades Made in the Shade 63
Snow Scraper, Guitar Shaker 67
The Blue Bonnet Racer 70
Fresh from the Farm 74
Summer of Regret and the
   Fist I Met 79
Trouble with the Townies 83
Two Points for Staying out
   of Trouble 88
The Three Ball Challenge 92
Thank You, Mrs. Crisman 96

Pitch, Please—But No
   Ants Allowed 100
Jack an Eye 104
The Giant Overpass 109
Barefoot on a Banana 113
The Jell-O® and Aunt Josie 117
Ode to the Party Line 121
The Look Arounds 124
Coach's Kid 129
Tane was Her Name 134
'Yes, Mrs. Bartholamew' 139

THE COLLEGE YEARS
The Loss of Someone I
   Never Knew 145
One-Swan Pond 148
Motor to the Meadow 151
Rise 'n' Shine, Dave 154
'You Wouldn't Dare' 158
Everyone Needs an Amy 162
Happy Birthday to Me 166
Something More Fragile
   Than Glass 170

THE ADULT YEARS
Lunch with the S&B Club 175
The Bike of My Youth 179
Livin' from One Country Song
   to Another 183
Ali and Me 186
Tannen: a Singer, a Wallflower,
   a Servant 190
With Todd, It was a Little Odd 194

THE EARLY YEARS

FIRST DAY OF SCHOOL AND A FURRY BATHROOM RUG

As school reopens each year, I think of the excitement of students entering a new grade and the anticipation of those starting school for the first time.

I remember my first day of school in '69. Because my mother was a teacher and was busy preparing for school herself, we didn't get all my supplies together until that very morning.

While we were racing around the house, we found the paste, scissors and some broken crayons. The crayons had rubbed together so often it was hard to tell

the original colors. Finally, we came to the last item on the list—the nap mat.

This seemed to puzzle my mother. For a moment she pondered, then dashed into the bathroom and picked up the lime-colored, furry rug that almost every American home has lying on the floor next to the bathtub. With the sack of supplies in my hand, she draped the furry rug over my shoulder and hustled me out the door where I took that fateful leap onto the big Blue Bird bus.

When I arrived safely at school, I expected to see my fellow classmates with big furry rugs hoisted over their shoulders . . . maybe one would have white, another blue or maybe red. Shoot! Not a furry rug in sight.

While kids stared at me, I realized what was "kindergarten hip" and what wasn't. A little boy named Artie was strutting around with what appeared to be a briefcase, but with a flip of the wrist, it sprung into a beautiful multi-colored nap mat. Boy, was I jealous! Another child had a pack of crayons with 487 colors and an electric sharpener that was so large she had to pull it on wheels and carry an extension cord around to use it.

The day, however, improved. The teacher was nice, and we colored. But during the introduction to show-

and-tell, we were on our nap mats (my furry rug) when little Jimmy chirped, "Maybe next show-and-tell Troy could bring his matching toilet seat cover."

Hey, that's okay! A few weeks later, when milk and cookies didn't agree with me, I threw up all over little Jimmy's lap. Oh, and that furry rug . . . well, as our nap pattern developed, it was "lights out" right after recess. Funny thing about those multi-colored nap mats that come in a briefcase—they're made of hard plastic. Combine that surface with sweaty skin—it's not a pleasant sensation. Soon they were calling out to me, "Hey, you wanna swap?"

Like an actor in a commercial, I propped my hands behind my head and said, "No thanks, guys. I feel good!"

I knew it was gonna be a great year.

THE KISS OF SPRING

It was the spring of '74, and I was a fourth-grader in elementary school. I remember it well for a couple of reasons. First, I got a Sears & Roebuck 3-speed bicycle that was fluorescent green with a sissy bar that scraped the sky. It had a banana seat long enough to hold me and five friends. Whether I was cruising in first gear or second, or riding like the wind in power third, my green and silver streamers danced in the wind—boy, was I cool!

Second, it was around this time that I started to notice a little neighbor girl named Darlene. She was one of my childhood friends, but this time it was different: I was in love. Soon, I found out that she shared my affections, and we became inseparable at recess and after school. In fact, in just three weeks, we were engaged to be married.

At times, I did have some doubts. I couldn't help but wonder if it was me she really liked, or was she just impressed with my incredibly cool bike (you know, the one with "power third")? Who could blame her? But this fear was laid to rest when I was grounded from my bike for two whole weeks for ramming it into my big brother's bike while he was still on it. Darlene proved faithful, and nothing changed.

I remember one recess in particular. We were playing atop the monkey bars when she leaned over and kissed me on the cheek. It was spontaneous; it was spring, and I was inspired. An honest look back would have revealed a kiss as dry as an autumn leaf, but I didn't care. I was in love, or so I thought.

By the time spring flowed into summer and summer into fall, we were passing in the hallways with an ordinary "hello." That's all right. I would write several "do you like me, circle yes or no" letters before my elementary school days were done.

As I grew older and the pressures and temptations of dating relationships weighed heavily, I would think fondly of those days: days of bike rides in the sun,

stomping through mud puddles in the rain, and stories and laughter under the clouds.

Sure, I was attracted to her. How could I not be? She was a vision of loveliness in her Girl Scout outfit. But it wasn't the handholding, or even the occasional kiss that meant so much. It was the excitement of the simple. I just needed to know I was okay.

THE HARLEY HOGS OF AMISH COUNTRY

It was summertime, and I was 16. I had been detasseling corn for the fourth summer in a row, and I'd managed to save a little money. Most of my friends were buying cars, but I didn't have enough cash, so I decided to get a little motorcycle instead. Besides, I didn't really need a car since the family Country Squire LTD Station Wagon, complete with side wood paneling, was at my disposal... and boy, what a great sound system! I could really jam to my 8-track of *The Bee Gees Live*.

I bought a little Kawasaki that was good both on the road and off. From that time on, I was riding the trails with friends or exploring in serene solitude my new frontier: the forgotten farms of Amish country. While

on one of these expeditions, I had an experience I'll never forget.

It was a soft summer Saturday, and I was rolling along at a modest 20 to 30 mph. With one hand gently adjusting the throttle, and the other planted on my knee, I looked to and fro, enjoying the beauty of all creation and the simple serenity of hand-tied bales drying in the hay fields. Suddenly, the scene was shattered as the breeze brought the menacing sounds of man's machinery, jolting me back to reality.

Peering down the road, I saw a bold parade of 30 to 40 Harley Davidsons cruising my way. The riders wore long hair and black leather vests; on their bare biceps they sported tattoos, probably mentioning "Mother." They looked as out of place in this "land that time forgot" as an Amish buggy would look rolling along a Los Angeles freeway at rush hour.

As the "hogs" rumbled toward me, fear entered my heart, and my mind began looking for an escape. Not only were they bearing down on me, they were covering the entire road. I was doomed. I practically closed my eyes, bracing myself. But wait . . . what was this? Slowly at first, then as if by choreography, the bikers began peeling off to make room for this skinny kid on a dirt bike. When I passed the first group of riders, my fear transformed to excitement. With fist clenched and elbow firm, I gave them the bikers' salute. As I continued on, one by one and two by two the leather-clad men returned my salute, sometimes with a slight smile.

Sure, I'm still embarrassed by my reaction of fear and prejudice. I had looked for a way out but couldn't find it. As a result, I experienced a thrill I remember to this day. I can't help but wonder how many times my fear and prejudices have kept me from the exhilaration of a shared moment with another human being—who appears to be very different from me—even though we're really a lot alike.

Well, I guess I'll never know. But, for a moment in time, "me and the boys" were brothers.

SWEET POTATO PANTS

It was August of 1970, and I was to be a first-grader in elementary school. Ah, first grade, school all day . . . lunch on a tray. I couldn't wait!

At first, lunch was all I'd dreamed it would be—food, friends and laughter. How I loved the lunch tray built with little sections for each food group. Because at six years of age, one thing you know is that food should never mingle with other food.

My favorite entree was the green Jell-O®. It was fun, full of flavor, and it could fly . . . well, at least with the help of a hard puff through a straw. There was something wonderful about the way Jell-O® wobbles in mid-air, almost as if in slow motion, and then—splat!—as it strikes its target with full force. This went on for a short time before I misfired at Jason Bobie and landed one just short of Miss Buller's foot. She handled it well, just before she "handled" the scruff of my neck into the kitchen where my sentence was quick and just—one week of cafeteria clean-up during recess.

Sure, I missed a whole week of dodge ball and kick ball, but I was guilty, and the punishment fit the crime. Soon, with lesson learned, lunchtime was fun again . . . until that day of the dreaded orange dish—sweet potatoes. I knew that anything that color should never meet my lips. That's one of the great things about being a kid: You need only to see the food article to judge its taste. Two lumps surrounded by a moat. Oozy and orange.

As I carried my tray back to the clean-up line, blood rushed to my face and I began to sweat, remembering the rule, "You must try everything on your plate." Quickly, I stirred up my cold, lumpy sweet potatoes in hopes of fooling Miss Buller, but she was a cafeteria veteran and that old trick wasn't going to work. "Take a bite of that sweet potato," she said calmly. Her stern persistence got the bite to my mouth, but no sooner had it entered than it shot back, unceremoniously, to the tray.

From that day on, the fear of this food ruined lunchtime for me. I had to find a way to hide those potatoes. At first, I would heave a helping under the

table, which worked until I hit Joey Wattenberger on the leg—then it was back to KP duty. One day I stumbled upon the solution: the milk carton. It was perfect. I always scrunched my carton down anyway, so why not shovel a few spoonfuls of sweet potato into the carton first?

This carried me through winter and most of spring, until I got a little careless one day and left a dab on top of the carton. Miss Buller had me open the carton, and there it was: lumpy and, by now, mixed with milk. Proud of her discovery, she happily handed me a spoon and said, "I want to see a big bite now."

What happened next is still a blur, but I knew I was in trouble. With just a few weeks of school remaining, I had exhausted all my options—my sane ones anyway.

The fateful day came the last week of school. I sat there silently as time ticked away. With all hope lost, I took a heaping spoonful, opened my front-left pocket, and shoved it in. Math class was miserable as I felt the warmth of the sweet potato against my leg. Even as the gloppy mess cooled, my stomach was every bit as queasy as if I'd eaten it.

Looking back, I know Miss Buller was trying to help me build strong bones and character, but I guess all of us, one way or another, must learn from our Sweet Potato Pants.

TROY KIDDER

THE COW PATTY CRUISER

It was in the fall of my fifth-grade year that I managed to get my dream machine: a minibike. This one came directly from my neighbor, Terry, who had entered junior high school and felt he was now too old for the minibike of his youth.

The homemade machine was a bargain beauty at $40 (money I had saved from mowing a few lawns). It had a mighty 3½-horsepower engine set in a standard bar frame, but that was just about its only traditional feature. Because Terry's mother was a seamstress, she made the seat and it was a masterpiece of construction. A foot thick and softer than any pillow I'd ever sat on, the seat was nearly a yard long and, like my father's LTD

Country Squire Station Wagon, could comfortably seat a family of six. Well, close to it anyway.

The 12 inches of foam had me riding high in the saddle, which might have looked a little odd since I was tall and thin, and it left me reaching down for the throttle. But that didn't bother me. I named her the "Comfort Cruiser," and we went everywhere together.

We rode the trails by the railroad tracks, kicked up dust on the country roads and buzzed around the barn when I was bored. But my favorite place to ride was the Millers' place next door. They had a field behind their shed where their son Roger and I had worn down an oval racetrack.

Roger and I enjoyed a good race. He rode a homemade three-wheeler that his dad had built. I, of course, piloted the "Cruiser."

Despite the challenges of the course, Roger handled his craft with skill. Though a mild-mannered young man, he wasn't afraid to bump up next to me at top speed. Challenges included the three or four cows that grazed within our oval. Besides the obvious obstacles that the cows daily deposited on our track were the cows themselves who, believe it or not, liked to play "chicken."

As we'd speed down the straight-aways, one or two of the cows would occasionally run down the path directly toward us. And since cows are not known for being quick-footed, we'd often have to veer to our right off the smooth trail and onto the bumpy field. One thing we soon discovered is that the cows always turned to their right as we got closer. As a result, the cows seldom slowed us down. After a while, they would stay in the middle of the oval and stand there with annoyed looks on their faces. (I guess cows always have annoyed looks on their faces.) I remember one autumn afternoon in particular when Roger and I were racing. The cows started out with their game of cow-chicken, but we ignored them, going on with our competition. As usual, the cows tired of the sport and opted for the middle of the oval. But as we started our last lap, the cows would have the last laugh.

I was right on Roger's tail as we entered the last curve. He was going so fast that his right-rear wheel came off the ground, spinning frantically. When the wheel came down, it landed on a fresh cow patty, shooting it directly back onto me ... SPLAT! SPLAT! SPLAT!

With Roger going on to victory, I skidded to a disoriented halt. My bare chest was covered, and a few fragments had caught my neck and cheek as well.

A few minutes later, in Roger's backyard, we laughed uncontrollably while he hosed me and my minibike down, now dubbed the "Cow Patty Cruiser."

As I look back and smile, I hope that if something out of the ordinary, something humbling, happens to me or you (whether at school, work or play), in the spirit of two young boys we can roll on the ground in laughter while a friend gets the hose.

OH, SAY CAN YOU SEE—
OR AT LEAST PLAY GUITAR

It was the spring of '76, and I was a sixth-grader at Millersburg Elementary School. Since school wouldn't be in session on July 4, we were having our bicentennial celebration early.

The program was to be a special evening performance in May for parents and community members. One day my role in the program suddenly increased. It was during one of our many practice sessions while singing "America, the Beautiful" that my buddy Greg blurted out, "This is boring . . . every song on piano! We need a rock 'n' roll guitar."

Miss Fields quickly fired back, "And just who, pray tell, will we get? Elvis?"

"No," said Greg calmly. "We'll get Troy."

My mouth dropped open, and I looked up at Miss Fields for her usual comeback to Greg's suggestions (which was "say hello to the chalkboard, young man"). But this time, she paused, pondered, then said, "Good idea."

Being a little unsure of myself—having never played in public—my vote was still for Elvis. But after a few moments of "Oh, please" from my classmates and a reassuring grip on the shoulder from my teacher, I was ready to make my debut. After all, I could play every song from my John Denver songbook almost flawlessly.

I brought my guitar (sorry, Greg: acoustic, not electric) to class every day for two weeks. I even practiced at home and was doing all right.

The excitement was mounting as the day approached. In History class, we learned about "Taxation without representation." We also learned about people yearning to live free to worship God as they saw fit—and we learned about courage.

Finally, the night arrived. I put on my red, white and blue bell-bottom pants three hours early, all the while tuning up my six-string. Elvis' loss was my gain, and my gain partially included Becky, who had not paid a whole lot of attention to me until my recent exploits in Music class. When I arrived, she was just as I imagined: red, white and blue bows tied to her pretty pigtails. She walked by me, smiled sweetly and said, "You'll be great!" Normally, this would have been enough to put a smile on my face for a week, but this night my mind was filled with something greater, something I couldn't quite put my finger on.

When the lights went down and all of us sixth-graders walked ceremoniously onto the gym floor unfolding a giant banner that read "America's Bicentennial 1776–1976," my hands began to tremble. It wasn't in fear of the crowd as I had imagined; it was a pride, a sense of purpose I'd not known before. It isn't easy for a sixth-grader to play guitar accompaniment with dignity, but that night I think I succeeded.

My bell-bottoms have long since worn out, with a solemn promise never to be worn again, and my John Denver songbook has been left to gather dust in my parents' basement. I hope, though, there's still room in my heart for "America, the Beautiful."

I LONG TO LIVE IN A NEIGHBORHOOD AGAIN

Jefferson Place was my neighborhood as a child. What a wonderful world it was, with woods nearby and a creek running through it. But best of all were my neighborhood friends.

Although the homes looked much the same—small ranch houses with evenly cut lawns—its occupants were very different. Across the street lived my best friend and constant companion, Mikey. He was shorter than most third-graders, but he was tougher too. And boy, did he have a passion for baseball. He played shortstop, and he would leap and dive and throw himself at any ball that dared to invade his territory. I also pitied anyone who might get in his way when he was running the bases.

Mikey wasn't perfect, but he wasn't mean either. Just like a lot of boys full of life, he was a bit misunderstood. I remember that Mikey disliked a boy named Ira almost as much as he loved baseball. He never explained why, and I guess I never really asked. Ira was a boy who lived on the corner lot by the creek. One day when he got off the bus, Mikey got off with him—and jumped on him. It took me and the bus driver to pull Mikey off Ira. The bus driver called Mikey's mother that night and that was the end of the feud—forever.

Steve was another good friend who lived just a few doors down. His dad was Mexican and his mom Amish, or at least she used to be. Steve's dad was cool; he had the admiration of us all when he would cruise his Harley Davidson chopper through the neighborhood. Steve's father also would let us watch him fly his remote-controlled airplane.

Steve's mother wasn't quite as helpful in the "cool" department. One day Steve was forced to get on the school bus with Dippity-do® on his hair. This would have spelled social ruin for most fourth-grade boys. And sure, we called him "Dippity-do head" for a couple of weeks, but Steve shrugged it off with grace. He was an endearing fellow who told the biggest lies ever heard and then would bet us $5 million that they were the

truth. In fact, he still owes me a couple of hundred million.

As unique as Steve may sound, Jay had everyone beat. He was as thin as a rail, which was partly due, we were told, to the fact that he was born with an upside-down heart with a hole in it and wasn't expected to live through his teens. But he seemed indifferent to his condition, and we seldom mentioned it.

Jay reminded me of a younger, naughtier Abe Lincoln. He stood as tall as any of us but was only in the second grade. He sported two buck teeth with a tremendous gap between the two. Jay held the neighborhood record for distance spitting, a title he carried with pride. He habitually used foul language, uttering phrases I'd never heard. And if you couldn't find Jay, he was probably down by the creek fishing, an ol' stogie hanging out of his mouth.

Jay was not at all athletic, but his sister Kim was. She was the first girl to play on our Little League baseball team and was a welcome addition to any team. Not only did she play, she made the all-star team two years running. Kim's athletic skills were not limited to baseball, as my neighborhood friends and I played many sports in a nearby empty lot—affectionately known as "the field."

It was here that my brother Todd, Kim's on-again-off-again boyfriend, was always captain. He picked the teams, and when we played football, he'd get down on one knee and draw plays in the dirt. I don't remember anyone ever complaining about him being captain all the time. Every team needs a captain, and he was ours. We understood that.

As for me, I was the kid who organized the games. It wasn't hard. No holiday was too special or time too sacred to call on my neighborhood pals. If someone had chores to do first, we all pitched in for the good of the team.

Somehow as we grow older, we have a way of letting our differences separate us. We seldom rally for the sake of the team. It seems we've forgotten that everyone has a part to play. Let's try to remember and work together—whether it costs us a few extra hours or a few extra dollars. This community is worth it! Yes, I long to live in a neighborhood again.

RISE TO THE OCCASION

At age 10, my suburban neighborhood was my world, and what a wonderful world it was. It had produced my first love and friends to fight for... friends who would fill a baseball field in five minutes flat.

I was an important piece of the puzzle. I knew my role and others' as well, and that's why I was devastated when my parents informed me that we were moving. They had purchased a house and some acreage 20 miles away just outside a small town. The town was Millersburg, Indiana. I started school in my new town with all the fifth-graders, and my fears were kept in check by staying uncharacteristically quiet those first few days at school; however, slipping quietly into my new environment was ruled out when word got out that I had played many sports in my old neighborhood. This brought a quick challenge from a confident Amish boy named LaVon. He was tall and thin and without question the outstanding athlete of his class. Nobody could run faster or throw a ball farther. My entrance put his status in question, and he naturally felt the need to remove all doubt.

After several sharp challenges from LaVon and some of his friends, I knew I couldn't back down. So we agreed on a game of one-on-one basketball to take place during the lunch hour the following day.

By the next morning every fifth-grader knew about the game. Tension was mounting. In fact, every time I looked at LaVon during math class he would point at himself, then me, and mouth the words, "I can beat you!"

It was the moment of truth . . . lunch time. After we both filled up on potato boats, green beans, applesauce and a cookie, we were off to the playground with 15 or so classmates following behind. The first player to 20 points, or whoever was ahead when recess ended, would be declared the winner.

LaVon got the ball first since it was his home court, and he drove easily to the basket and scored.

I could tell that the kids were already counting me out, but I quickly scored too. As we started exchanging baskets, the excitement in the crowd began building, along with the numbers of kids circling the basketball court.

Eventually, the score was knotted at 18, and I had the ball. Glancing at Mrs. Riley, the playground supervisor, who was fumbling in her pocket for her whistle, I knew that recess time was short. So I quickly made a move toward the basket, but LaVon cut me off. I took two dribbles back toward the free-throw line, rotated my body and launched an ol' hook shot my father had taught me. The ball climbed high in the air and, at its peak, I heard the whistle blow in the distance. The ball seemed to hang there for a second, and then it crashed with force through the chain net.

The kids exploded with yells and hollers, and LaVon and I walked off the court arm in arm, surrounded by the cheers of our peers.

Sure, it's always great to win, but this game wasn't so much about winning or losing, as I later discovered, but about facing challenges and earning respect. As I grow older, I find myself in similar situations—situations that a good hook shot can't resolve. What it comes down to then is honor, courage and dedication.

Win or lose, let's "give it all we got" and rise to the occasion.

A BOY AND HIS REX

Like many boys at age 12, I wanted a dog of my own—a big dog. One that would go hunting and fishing with me whenever I wanted. A friend to jog alongside when I rode my bike to town or chase me when I buzzed my minibike around our small farm.

One summer afternoon I got my wish as my Mom pulled into the driveway with a large Irish Setter in the backseat of the family's Country Squire Station Wagon. He was a beauty, with long red hair, stout chest and intelligent eyes. He jumped out of the car right on top of me. With

his paws on my shoulders, we looked eye to eye, and I knew instantly that we would be best friends.

My Mom opened the back door of the house, and Rex ran into the kitchen and automatically—in one bite— devoured my bologna sandwich from atop the counter. I looked at Mom and she looked at me, and we knew life at our house had just changed.

Despite that episode, Rex had already been well trained at an obedience school and had spent his first few years as a quiet companion for an elderly lady. For some reason the lady had to move, and that's how my Mom got him. He seemed happy to be with us. He could now run free with me, and from that time on, he and I were inseparable.

That summer we did all the things I dreamed we'd do. Rex loved my friends, and they enjoyed him, except when we played hide-and-seek at night. With Rex's help, I literally couldn't lose. Even Saturday morning cartoons were more fun as I would awaken early, often with Rex's cold, wet nose nudging my arm, and we would eat egg sandwiches together and watch TV. I drew the line, though, at sharing my chocolate milk.

When summer ended and I was back in school, Rex would wait on the front porch for me every day when I got off the bus. After wrestling in the backyard, we would sit on the porch and I would tell him about my day as he licked me and playfully bit my wrists; nipping was his way of showing affection.

And occasionally, on autumn nights some of the neighbor boys would come over and play football in the backyard. Rex always enjoyed barking from the sidelines—although when someone got tackled, he couldn't resist leaping on top of the pile and lightly biting whatever body part he could reach with his teeth. The other kids would laugh and yell and often try to tackle him.

Winter with Rex was even better as he loved to jump and play in the snow and chase us as we raced down the hill on our sleds. And at night he would curl up at the end of my bed. The added warmth was much appreciated because our old farmhouse didn't have heat upstairs. Even so, I would awaken in the middle of the night, and Rex would be stretched out next to me, snoring away. His 65-pound body had me pinned against the wall; sometimes I would elbow him because he barely left me any room to move. He would awaken, get up slowly, then plop down in protest on the wooden floor in the hallway. But when morning came, all was forgiven, and we were off together.

When spring came I was already looking forward to an entire summer with Rex. Unfortunately, a mysterious illness took away his health and happiness, and he died before summer arrived. Of course, my parents offered me another dog, but I just couldn't accept a replacement.

As I slowly managed to let Rex go, I came to realize that no friendship is replaceable. And if an animal that cost me nothing cannot be replaced, how much more important is a relationship with a fellow human being? Let's resolve to treasure all of our friendships.

BIG BOOTS, BIG HEART

Randy Hite was one of my childhood friends. He wasn't any taller than the rest of us third-graders, but he had a short body and unusually long legs. Randy always wore cowboy boots that sort of flopped along at the end of his rubbery legs.

Although Randy lived in Texas only until he was two, he talked with a slow drawl like his daddy. His father was his hero, which made it unspeakably sad when he was killed that year, having fallen from atop a silo at work.

Randy missed only a few days of school, but it took several months before we really began to relate again. I

remember when Randy surprised the whole gang with an invitation to a slumber party at his house. About 10 of us rode the bus home with him on a Friday night.

We had pizza and ice cream; we played kickball and tag. What a night. I remember his Mom as well. She was much too pretty, we thought, to be the mother of someone we knew. It turns out she was understanding, too, as we would soon discover.

As Calpurnia says about some young boys in the novel *To Kill a Mockingbird,* we got the "look arounds" about 1 a.m. and, from Randy's top bunk bed, climbed through his bedroom window into the darkness of the night. We quickly got caught in a rainstorm and scrambled back in the window as fast as we could.

With six or seven wiggling, squirrelly third-graders on top of the bed, it gave way and crashed with a loud thud, breaking into several pieces. Randy's mother rushed in, and there we were: wet little boys sitting on a busted bed. We braced ourselves for the worst, only to hear, "You boys better get some towels."

As third grade came to a close, I had spent the night at Randy's several times—just the two of us. We had become great friends. Randy always had been a gentle soul. But since his father's death, he had a humility, a wisdom, that went beyond his 10 years. Yet he still managed to maintain the freshness of childhood.

I'll never forget the last night we would hang out together before Randy and his Mom moved back to Texas to be near family. We were up even later than usual into the wee hours of the morning.

I was pecking away at a little red typewriter that Randy had, and he was drawing pictures of badges—a badge that he would one day wear with pride. Randy wanted to be a firefighter. He wanted to help people. And in the dark hours he dug down deep and said, "Maybe I can save someone like my dad. Someone who got caught in a jam."

After a moment of silence, Randy's comment gave me the courage to share what others would only laugh at in the daylight: "I want to be a writer. I want to write stuff that makes a difference."

Randy didn't say anything. He only nodded quietly, and I felt it was okay. It was these nights, with adults safely in bed, that we loved as children, because no one was around to douse the fires of our dreams with the cold water of their reality.

I believe that Randy's reality is just what he said it would be: He's down there in Texas fighting fires and saving folks who are "in a jam."

Thank God for the faithful souls like Randy, who aren't afraid to search their hearts to find their calling—and still have the grace to encourage others to do the same.

TROY KIDDER

THE SOLE OF A SHOE AND THE SOUL OF A BOY

It was like any other summer day for this 9-year-old boy and his older brother. The "gang" was meeting us at our house after lunch, from whence we would proceed to the field for our daily ritual—baseball.

As Mom made our bologna sandwiches, our routine was interrupted by her sudden discovery of my brother Todd's sneakers. His toes were sticking out, and they made a "flopping" sound as he walked across the kitchen.

My mother was horrified. She quickly declared, "No child of mine is going to run around the neighborhood looking like that." Before Todd could utter even two words of protest, Mom had him in the family's Country

Squire Station Wagon heading straight for the shoe store. If she'd only known how hard Todd had to work on those shoes to get them just the way he wanted them.

In the meantime, I finished my sandwich and began to look for something to do until Mom returned with our all-time pitcher. I pulled out my six-string acoustic guitar and began to play right there in the living room.

As I engrossed myself in the melody of my music, I had forgotten about the baseball game until the doorbell rang, and there were Mark, Kim, Steve and Mikey—hands cupped around their curious little faces—peering through the screen door, wondering what in the world I was doing. Since no friends were allowed in our house when our parents were gone, I was startled and yelled out to them, "Todd's not here; he'll be back in a little bit."

Kim asked, "What's going on in there?" By now the rest of the gang had arrived—all 11 or 12 of them were on our front porch, crowded around the front door, trying to look in. Kim continued, "Why don't you play us a song?" A little shy and unsure of myself, I said, "No, you don't want to hear me play." Quickly, voices rang out: "Sure we do." "Yeah!" "Come on." "Please!"

Inspired by the enthusiasm, I strummed one of the three chords I knew, and my audience got quiet. I turned to the side a bit so that I didn't have to see them; before long I was into my spontaneous song. I began to make up words for this makeshift tune. They just poured out, seemingly without even going through my head. I strummed harder as I found a chorus and stayed with it. I even began to move to the rhythm. Finally, without forethought, the song ended. There was a quiet pause, and then my friends on the porch burst into applause.

As if on cue, my mother and brother rolled into the driveway. I put aside my six-string, picked up my ball glove and opened the front door to numerous slaps on the back and salutations. I walked to the station wagon to greet my brother, who looked somewhat perplexed in his new Converse "The Winner" sneakers.

Before anyone else could say anything, Kim blurted to Todd, "Wow, you missed it! You should have heard your brother!" And together we went off to play baseball with scarcely a mention of it again.

It wasn't a big moment in my life, but it has stayed with me. Maybe it was because, for a short time, I did something few of us do, especially as we grow older. I put myself on the line. It was almost as if I held my heart out in my hand and said, "Here it is."

The appreciation that I felt from my friends seemed more because of my willingness to bare my soul—to be

vulnerable for a moment—than the performance itself. I wonder . . .

THE SONG OF SUMMER

Oh, summer as a child—simple, yet full, and there was always something to do. Summer and songs met on the way to Little League baseball games. Three or four of us walking arm in arm, we sang: "We are the Angels, the mighty Angels. We fight for our team. We fight for our name."

We sang as we rode our bikes down the middle of the street. You could hear us five blocks away. They were made-up songs—songs about each other and songs about great adventures and, of course, silly songs of joy and friendship.

We played by the creek, fishing and sometimes just splashing and laughing. There was life and freedom in the woods. A world of our own as children.

And sometimes when Mikey, Jay and the others were caught in their own wonder, I would quickly take Darlene by the hand and we would escape through the trees. With backs bowed and eyes to the skies, we'd dance and twirl as the summer sun showered us through the leaves. Oh, the passion and innocence of a first love.

At night, under the starry wonders, we would play hide-and-seek. The lighted porch was home base. I can still feel the nervousness in my stomach as my time was short to find a good hiding place. The numbers in the night echoed ever closer: "17, 18, 19, 20 . . . ready or not, here I come." We played deep into the darkness as the dew began to settle on the ground.

Finally, another song rang out from any number of parents: "Jeffrey, Kim, Jay, it's time to come home." All hiding places were immediately evacuated as we ran for our houses.

Safe at home, we were tucked in with prayers and stories, and sometimes Dad would take us off to bed with my brother and me hanging off each shoulder.

Slumber was sweet but short, since summer days started early, and my eyelids could hold back the sunlight no longer. I leaped from bed, grabbed a Pop-Tart and was off to Mikey's across the street, shouting my arrival all the way—but now, how do we start the day?

Childhood is but the beginning. We must continue to grow, explore and discover, for this is the essence of life. Let's not forget the excitement of the simple: It's relationship with others. It's bike rides in the sun, stomping through mud puddles in the rain, and stories and laughter under the clouds.

So sing it out—life is good and we have so much to learn and look forward to.

DRIFTING LIKE SNOW

I remember the summer that we left our small suburban home for a place in the country. I was 10 years old and not in total agreement with the move. To ease the pain of leaving my friends, my parents promised that I could get a "big dog." It was something I had always wanted, and they knew it.

Within weeks of relocating, we saw an ad in the paper for a white German Shepherd. "Free," it said. Perfect. I'd always wanted a German Shepherd (not necessarily white), and the cost was certainly in my parents' price range.

We visited the farm to see the dog. He was furry and white, all right, but there were some surprises. The farmer who'd placed the ad had found the animal while out plowing his field. The dog was hobbling along with a lame front leg and bruises and tears on his body. One of his ears looked like something or someone had tried to rip it off.

The farmer just wanted to find him a good home, and our family passed the test. I named him "Snow," and we rode home together in my parents' red LTD station wagon. Snow and I sat in the back and got acquainted. He licked my face, and I was careful not to bump his sore paw.

It became obvious that Snow had been beaten, and he was a little timid around others, but he began to trust me and, slowly, he warmed up to our entire family.

That summer we put salve on his sore leg, and he healed quickly. The other spots healed as well, and he was beautiful, with thick, white fur and bright eyes. We ran and played together, and when I rode my bike he ran alongside. But as Snow got healthier, I became disappointed in him. Even though he would now walk up to "strangers" who pulled into the driveway, he didn't bark.

Sure, he looked good, and we could play together, but he wasn't what I had dreamed of. He lacked something inside. When I had thought of a big dog, I had thought of a bark—a deep, dark, aggressive bark that said, "Beware, big scare." One of power and strength.

I didn't want a mean dog, just one that meant business when strangers happened by. One that sent a message that something or someone important lives here—and you'd better watch your step.

I think of all of us: Sure, we have been hurt too. Maybe someone has tried to rip off one of your ears. But after you find that safe place, and your eyes become bright and your coat thick and beautiful, will you get your bark back? You know, that thing that makes the difference between just getting by and forcefully advancing.

Well, as I lost interest in Snow, he began to drift. He roamed to other farms, and we had to get rid of him. It may sound surprising, but I really didn't miss him that much. But I did go on struggling those next few years with loneliness and insecurity.

I can't help but wonder what would have happened if Snow had gotten his bark back . . . if he would have become strong. I can't help but believe that I would have been stronger too. I guess I'll never know for sure, but I learned something important . . .

I learned that it's not the thick, furry coat and the bright eyes that make the difference in us as human beings either. It's our "bark"—the fire inside that makes the difference. Not only in our lives, but in the lives of those around us, including the ones we love.

BACK TO THE TREE TRUNK

Kindergarten was great. We finger-painted colorful worlds with splashes of movement and light—no lines to limit our creativity. We baked peanut butter cookies together. We held hands and sang songs, but now I was six and ready for more. I wanted to read and write.

Ahhh, school all day, lunch on a tray; I couldn't wait! I met our first-grade teacher, Mrs. Yoder, on the first day of school. She was very thin and stood not much taller than her pupils. To my first-grade eyes, her age was about 90. But she carried herself like a drill sergeant, and you dared not cross her. It was clear to all of us that the party was over, and we had been enlisted into her world of education.

I remember that in just a few days' time we were already reading about the adventures of two siblings named Dick and Jane. The stories were okay, but I wanted to write. Finally, I got my wish; however, writing was much different than I had anticipated.

The pencils given us resembled stout tree trunks. They were so big, in fact, that Mrs. Yoder had to cart them in on a wheelbarrow. And with our tiny fingers, it took both hands to pick them up. I could barely lift the pencil, let alone write with it. Through determination, though, I finally positioned the pencil so that I could make a writing motion and, just as I was getting some hope again, Mrs. Yoder passed out the paper.

It was brown with fat dotted lines and the wood chunks still in it. One tablet took up the entire desk. If it got knocked off your tabletop, you'd better watch your foot.

The paper was rough and tough to write on. The worst was the little chunks of wood. Just as I finally got a little rhythm going, I would hit one of those chunks, which would knock me out of whack. I'll never forget the awful accident that happened at the desk to my right. We were a few weeks into our writing, and many of us were still struggling, but despite the many challenges, Jason Bobie had caught on quickly and was writing faster than anyone. He was speeding along one day while writing in cursive when he hit a bigger than usual wood chunk. It was terrible. I can still see the withering look of pain on his face. Jason was in a shoulder harness for weeks.

I finally decided there had to be a better way. So I asked my older, cooler brother, Todd, who was in third grade, what to do. He went and got a No. 2 pencil and slid it into my hand. He said, "Write!" So I did.

I said, "Ahhh, ohhh! That's nice!"

Smiling, Todd added, "That's what we use in third grade." Then he said, "Listen, the next time the "ol' battle ax" is walking up and down the rows, wait 'til she gets on the other side of the room, then shove your tree trunk under the lid of your desk and start writing with your No. 2. And when she comes back, start writing with the tree trunk again. It's simple!"

I said, "Boy, you're cool!" He said, "I know."

Well, the next day, I did just what he said. Mrs. Yoder was patrolling as always and, as she got to the other side of the room, I pulled out my No. 2 and got rolling. Careful not to hit the wood chunks, I was flying—having a ball. So much so that I forgot about the teacher. Suddenly, I felt a sensation that someone was standing behind me. I knew it was Mrs. Yoder. I dared not move.

She began to shake. I could see her out of the corner of my eye. The veins in her neck flared and then I heard a high, shrieking voice exclaim:

"Nummmmberrr twoooo!"

The next thing I knew, I was jolted up out of my seat as we stood face to face. Eyes bulging and veins still throbbing, she continued to express herself on the matter: "Who do you think you are to bring this in without my permission?!"

I know she said more, but that's all I can bear to remember. However, she was right; the lesson lives on.

I never pretended to understand the tree trunks. I still don't. But she was the professional, not I. She had a strategy. I was just confused and inconvenienced. Although it's not wrong to ask questions, sometimes it's even better to work hard and have faith.

By the way, I went on to receive a certificate for excellent penmanship that year. And Mrs. Yoder . . . she got younger and nicer as the year went on. Go figure.

A SHOT AT HISTORY

When I think back to my time in high school, I have very few regrets. But if I could change just one thing, I know what it would be. And this one thing, this one situation, doesn't mean that much now, but it may have changed my life and the lives of others—for the better.

My junior year in high school I was a quirky kid standing 6 feet tall and weighing only 130 pounds. Having some athletic skills, I worked my way to sixth man on the basketball team in the heart of roundball country—Indiana. The fourth game of the season we were undefeated and playing a much larger inner-city

school that also was undefeated but ranked 16th in the state.

Often throughout the game I was called upon to bring the ball up court against an aggressive full-court press. I would dribble behind my back and between my legs. I would slow down, only to speed up again. And on occasion, I would take a slow, giant step directly toward the face of my opponent, then take off again as fast as I could.

All this seemed to be working, as I didn't lose the ball even once. However, the game was close and, despite my dribbling exhibition, I hadn't been able to make a shot from the field or the foul line.

With just four seconds left in the game, we were down one point. We had the ball under our own basket, and the play called for me to receive the ball on the in-bounds pass, dribble toward the basket, then kick it back to our best shooter for a 2-pointer just beyond the foul line.

The play almost worked. I caught the ball and took a dribble, but immediately the whistle blew, and a foul was called: reaching in on the defense. "One and one": make the first and you get a second.

I was escorted to the foul line by my reassuring teammates and, as I was waiting to receive the ball from the ref, I noticed the crowd for the first time. Our 1,500-capacity gym was packed with people. In fact, they were even spilling out of the entryways, not to mention the policemen, principals and school administrators who surrounded our floor just steps away from the court.

I thought to myself, "I can't miss this shot." And in my mind I couldn't imagine missing. I received the ball. I took more time than usual bouncing the ball at the foul line. Finally, it was off my fingertips. It didn't feel quite right, but I had concentrated so strongly that I knew it had to go in; and it did. The crowd exploded with cheers.

The score was tied and, just as quickly as the crowd rose up in jubilation, it hushed and shushed as I was given the ball for the potential game winner. I took a deep breath and launched the second one, which felt good, looked good, but "clank," horn, "too bad," overtime. We went on to lose that night in double overtime.

Now, you may be thinking that the one situation of high school that I would change would've been to make that shot. That's not it! Well, not totally. If I were to do it all over again, I would receive the ball from the ref for that second shot, eye the basket for a moment, turn around with my back to the basket, and I would launch

a one-handed, behind-the-head free throw that I had practiced countless times at my barn basket on many a starry night. If I make it, I'm ushered into Hoosier folklore forever, and if I miss it, I'm also ushered into Hoosier folklore. But that's not even the point. Sure, I would have enjoyed it for a few days, but certainly it wouldn't mean much beyond that. No. My purpose here is greater.

That shot could've unlocked the creativity in me. It could've unlocked the creativity in any number of those 1,500 fans. A passion and expression that go well beyond just sports and a moment of entertainment. We're talking a far-reaching lifestyle change.

It's the throwing off of fear and the tearing apart of the everyday mindsets that take us into a life of wonder and purpose. Think of the life that could be lived. Think of the problems that could be solved. Think of the joy.

No, I can't go back and take that shot over again. Would I really do that? You bet I would! And I'll prove it a hundred different ways every day of my life from here on—and you can too.

So go ahead, get in the game, take your shot and remember: Miss or make, win or lose, you're taking a shot that few dare take.

TROY KIDDER

THE 'MARK' OF OUR NEIGHBORHOOD

Mark was one of my friends. While he wasn't a "pal," I liked him. But he was the closest thing we had to a "neighborhood bully."

That title was more for size than merit, even though he did get my big brother down one time and refused to let him up. I stood there screaming at Mark until he finally relented.

Mark did prove tough on the football field, and no matter whether he was chasing and tackling, walking the halls of Jefferson Elementary, or (I'm told) going to church, you could be sure he'd be wearing his No. 51 Chicago Bears jersey—a solemn tribute to his all-time favorite football player, Dick Butkus.

The fact that Mark wore the same football jersey every day of his life wouldn't qualify him for uniqueness, at least in our neighborhood. There were, however, other oddities that made Mark "Mark." Some, of course, he had nothing to do with. His dad was a truck driver who drove 18-wheelers and the biggest Cadillacs you'd ever seen. Even though we lived in that neighborhood just three years, I remember several "Caddies": a yellow one, a black one, a different yellow one and a bright green one.

His dad wasn't around much due to his trade, which left his short and very slender Mom driving the mammoth steel beauty from Detroit. As she rounded the corner and headed for home, sometimes it seemed the car was driving itself until she got close enough for me to see her head peeking just above the steering wheel.

Mark's family lived in a yellow house that may have been a tad smaller than their automobile. And they had a huge CB tower that scraped the sky. In fact, Mark used to brag that a few times his father had received signals from Japan. It's not that I doubt the truthfulness of my old friend—but do Japanese truck drivers even have CBs? Once in a while I would go over to Mark's house to play. Though there was very little room upstairs in their home, the basement had a giant Lionel train setup, which pretty much covered the entire cement-walled room. It was always dark and cold down there, but we didn't mind and played for hours. Though Mark loved his trains, he always let me be the main engineer when I came over.

As we headed back upstairs into the light, it never failed: Johnny Cash would be playing boldly on the hi-fi, the bass rumbling so loudly that the entire house would shake. I can still hear it and feel it. Oh, how such memories stay with us through the years.

I don't know how much of an impact Mark and his family had on me. I have yet to talk on a CB, I don't drive a Cadillac, and, to this day, I haven't purchased any of Johnny Cash's music. However, maybe just being able to spend some time with someone who approaches life a little differently was enough. And, who knows, maybe Mark's family saw some oddities in me too.

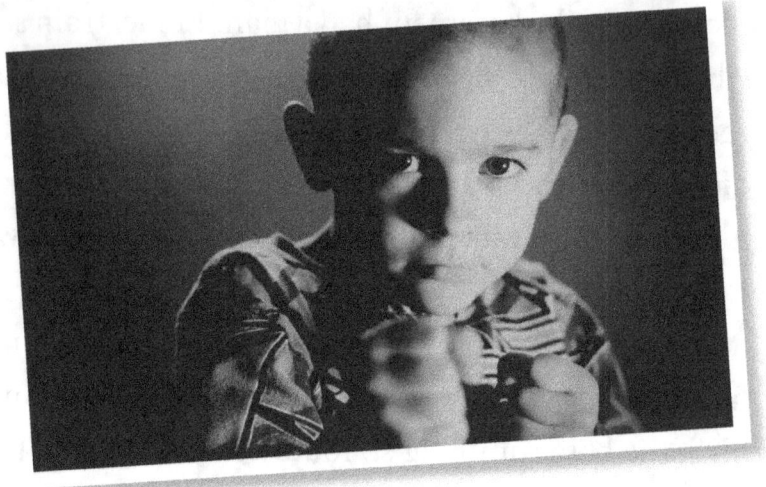

THE SPANK

Joe Sanders was my fifth-grade History teacher and basketball coach at Millersburg Elementary. Although Coach Sanders exhibited a delightful sense of humor with his fellow instructors (and, on occasion, in the classroom or on the practice field), he was the type of teacher who could make a student, me included, shake from nothing more than a stern look.

The coach's intimidating features went well beyond his 6-foot-1, 260-pound (or so) frame. His bald head and round cheeks were highlighted by a large mustache that curled at both ends. And while he lectured, Mr. Sanders often reached into his pocket, pulled out a small, round container of wax and began stroking the curls of his mustache.

Coach had short, stubby fingers. While that in itself was noticeable to a fifth-grader, the fact that he wore rings on nearly every one of those fingers highlighted them even more. Any of the rings easily could've served as a bracelet for our developing wrists.

The rings were hard to miss, as Mr. Sanders often sat at his desk during our "quiet" study time absentmindedly rubbing his hands together with a "clicking" sound, the rings striking one another with each stroke.

I'll never forget a particular day in Mr. Sanders' class. He was lecturing on one of the finer points of American history while flipping the corners of his mustache. He said something that caught my attention, and a funny comment entered my mind. Without thinking, I blurted it out, much to everyone's surprise—including my own. Immediately Mr. Sanders stopped what he was saying and loudly inquired, "Who said that?"

Of course, every finger quickly pointed my direction. Coach then barked at me like a drill sergeant: "Kidder, did you say that?!" (Coaches often call you by your last name.)

Now sunken slightly in my chair, I nodded and squeaked out a plaintive "yes."

Mr. Sanders stared at me for a moment, then turned away. When he looked back, I saw a slight smile come over his face, and he said, "That was pretty funny."

The class and I exhaled together in one big sigh of relief, and we went back to work. But I began to think a lot about that moment: Joe Sanders thought I was funny. I felt a new kinship with my teacher, almost a sense of being "buddies," though I still would never call him by his first name—at least to his face—and expect to live.

A few weeks had gone by, and I was now looking for another chance to delight my history teacher. Finally, my opening came. It seemed just like the other time. The class was quiet. Mr. Sanders was talking and curling (you know, the mustache). When he finally said something into which I thought I could insert my humor, I spoke up with confidence.

This time, however, it was as if he was waiting for it: "Kidder, to the office!" Which, to my dismay, was next door. He followed me in and picked up the classic wooden paddle, complete with large holes in it.

Before I knew it, I was grabbing my ankles, and he was whopping me so hard that it echoed through the halls of the old brown-bricked school. Next thing I knew, I was back at my second-row desk, wiping tears from my eyes and wondering what in the world had just happened.

Admittedly, I was confused at first. The situations seemed the same to me. But they weren't. The first time was an accident—an honest, spontaneous thing that happened. Fortunately he found it funny and "grace was shed on me." The next time, though, I was looking for an opportunity to break the rules, and I received quick and just punishment.

Whether Mr. Sanders really understood what had gone on in these two situations, I don't know. I suspect he did. But the spank taught me that although situations sometimes appear the same, they may be very different. In the end, it all comes down to this: What really matters is the intent of the heart.

PRETEND PUPS FOR SALE

Ah, first grade! School all day, lunch on a tray. What can I say? It was grand. Next to lunch and gym, "Show and Tell" was my favorite time.

I loved to see what other kids had and what they were doing. My imagination would run wild as my classmates shared about their father being a fireman, doctor or heavy-equipment operator—and they had the pictures to prove it. Greg Eash even brought in his dad's official police officer cap. Wow!

Others talked about their relatives, their homes and cars, their toys and trips. But what did I have?

Then it finally happened. It was an ordinary Show and Tell Tuesday, right after Christine told about her much older brother joining the Navy. She even had a duffel bag that said "NAVY" stamped in large letters right on it.

I could take it no more. I jumped to my feet and called out, "Mrs. Yoder! Mrs. Yoder! I have something."

Taking note of my enthusiasm, she graciously said, "Come up front, Troy, and please share this exciting news." Before I knew it, I had told the class that we had a litter of puppies—10, to be exact. I continued, "And there are brown ones and black ones and brown and black ones. And even a little tan one I named Koala, since she looks like a bear."

It was wonderful. My classmates were oohing and ahhing, wiggling and giggling. And then the request rang out: "I want one!"

"Yeah, I want one too!" And without thinking I blurted back, "50 cents. 50 cents for a puppy."

Now that I had stirred the class into a complete frenzy, Mrs. Yoder had to step in to restore order: "Okay, okay, class. Settle down. Troy has pups for sale. You can talk with him during recess about it. But remember to ask Dad and Mom before anything is decided."

I was feeling so good that it didn't really hit me, at least not very hard, that I had put myself in quite a predicament. Not only would I fail to produce puppies,

I didn't even have a dog ... male or female. I had thought the whole thing would pass, but it didn't.

The very next day, kids were bringing me 50 cents— sometimes two quarters, sometimes pennies and nickels— and by the end of the day, I had quite a stash. (I didn't know what else to do, so I took the money.)

This worked fine with the excitement still high and me the center of attention for three days. It sounds funny now, but in my first-grade mind it never really occurred to me that somehow this had to end—and end badly for me. Well, that third night or so, my buddy Bruce's mom, Mrs. Buller, who worked in the school cafeteria, called my Mom and wanted to pick up "their" puppy. My mother was perplexed to say the least.

Funny thing, I don't remember the punishment or even if there was one. I don't recall returning the money, though I'm sure my parents saw to it. And I don't remember how the kids treated me after they found out the truth. (Kids are much more forgiving than adults in those situations anyway.)

I just have a fond memory. Sure, I knew deep down that what I did was wrong. But my heart wasn't set to deceive anyone. I just wanted to have something that nobody else had—something others admired and could enjoy with me. I guess all of us need that from time to time.

TRADES MADE IN THE SHADE

I was always "wheeling and dealing" as a child. At age 11 or 12, there wasn't much money to be had . . . I just enjoyed the sport of it—the fun of having something different, not necessarily better.

I recall one string of trades made the summer before sixth grade. I began with a Sears & Roebuck 3-speed bike that had been discarded by my older brother years earlier. This silver wonder shone like chrome and, though the gears were "function free" (that's slick-salesman talk for "they don't work"), the single-speed bike was still a sought-after commodity.

Finally an older boy from the other side of town—the side I wasn't allowed on very often—offered me his bike in exchange for the chrome beauty. His was a small yellow bicycle with one gear. However, he had made it into a "chopper" (front wheel extended), and I could see myself moving the throttle and making loud rumbling noises, my lips protruding and vibrating exuberantly, while proudly rolling down the street. I could play "motorcycle gang." Deal!

As much as I loved the new machine, on my way home I ran into Steve, who also coveted the yellow bike. Under a large shade tree we began to barter. But alas, it seemed no deal was possible. After he offered me his 3-speed purple Huffy, I shook my head, got on my machine and fired up my lips to leave. But before I could get out even one rumble to "blow this popsicle stand" (that's motorcycle-gang talk for "leave quickly"), he said, "Wait, I got it!"

In a flash Steve rushed into his house and, even before the screen door could crash back against the doorframe, he returned with his family's brand-new air rifle. It shot BBs and pellets. Seeing me wiping the drool from my chin, Steve knew he had a deal. So I sauntered home an armed man.

Though I had "rumbled" barely five minutes on my new bike, I did manage to do some damage with that gun: barn windows, unsuspecting sparrows and a few misfires at the neighbor's cat. A couple of days later, though, I ran into Marty, Steve's older brother. It seems Marty had plans for the air rifle and wanted it back. This time I was determined to keep my new prize until... the go-kart rolled out of the shed. Wow! What a beauty: low to the ground, slick tires and a mighty 3½-horsepower engine. Marty told me it didn't always start. He was right. We tried, it didn't. However, I had to have it. For the air rifle and $20 cash on the barrelhead (all the money I had in the world), I was soon pushing my go-kart home.

I don't recall what happened to that thing. It only started once the whole time I had it, but I enjoyed just sitting on it in the barn. Cool.

It's funny. When we were kids we were more honest, more willing to ask, to try, to be. Lately I haven't tried to trade my neighbor my Montgomery Ward "YardMaster," with its puppy dog 12-horse engine, for his spanking-new 14-horse John Deere garden tractor, but suddenly I'm inspired. Let's talk.

Who knows, maybe I have something else to throw in to close the deal—something he has always longed for, like my Save Mart "Sensational Seven" rake set.

Could it be that part of the thrill of childhood trades—bikes, BB guns and baseball cards or beads, buttons and Barbie dolls—was relationship? The joy of life was when something new (or different) was more important than clinging onto possessions so tightly.

TROY KIDDER

SNOW SCRAPER, GUITAR SHAKER

I suppose we've all done it one way or another. I mean dream or pretend certain things when we were young—things that were so real then yet seem so silly now.

I confess... one of my oddest infatuations occurred quite frequently when I rode in my parents' baby-blue '69 Chevy Impala. I was but six or seven years old, but I knew what I wanted to be, and I had no doubt that I could do it—so why wait?

I wanted to be a rock 'n' roller on the radio. Sure, I played guitar and by then I already knew several songs and a couple of chords. But "Go Tell Aunt Rhody" and "London Bridges" weren't gonna cut it. I wanted some "real" stuff. So if reality wouldn't do, why not create a world that would? And that world opened up to me in the back seat of my parents' Chevy. Whether we were skipping

across town for some groceries, heading to Grandma's for goodies or on a summer vacation, I lived another life.

All dreams need props, and for me, it was the illustrious snow scraper that my parents kept in the back seat of the car—through all seasons regardless. This scraper, my guitar, fit my arms perfectly. The red and blue bristles were the strings, and the plastic handle was the neck.

I would strum the "strings" with strength while moving my left hand deliberately up and down the "neck." I would play beautiful ballads and foot-stompin' dance tunes and good ol' rock 'n' roll. And if my parents didn't oblige (which they usually didn't) by playing the radio to help me along, then I heard the songs in my head just as clearly.

I remember going past many cars, cars that I just knew had their radio on. I would peek my head up past the door handle, tilt my chin just high enough to clear the bottom of the window and, as anyone dared to look at me, I smiled as if to say, "Hey, that's me! I'm playing on your radio." Then I would put my head back down and go at it even harder.

I remember the thrill, the excitement—the kind of stirring you can feel only when you believe it in your heart. And I did. I truly believed.

Sure, it was my childish imagination. But what I felt was real. I had something. Just like those on the radio who boast their vocals boldly, screech of loves lost and wail about mountains to climb. I wasn't sure what all that meant, but I felt the emotion: the longings of love, passion and pain—even joy.

Why the snow scraper and rock 'n' roll? I guess I felt so much more from the musicians and singers than from those around me at the time. I was crying out (mostly inside, to be sure) to hear and be heard.

But I'm starting to realize that we don't all have to be poets or performers; we're people. We have our lives to live and stories to tell. They may just be a little locked up, that's all.

Do what you gotta do. Crawl to the back seat of your Impala, find that snow scraper and begin to play. And you'll no doubt find some feelings too: feelings of faith and fear, fight and fun—but find 'em!

And as you peek your head above the door handle and tilt your chin just high enough to clear the bottom of the window, you may find there are plenty of passersby just waiting for someone bold enough and brave enough to share a foot-stompin' or tear-jerkin' song of the heart.

THE BLUE BONNET RACER

It may sound odd, but I had a mower as a child—and not just any mower. This one boasted a solid metal frame with a mighty 5-horsepower engine. "Mower," however, was a misnomer since no mowing deck had ever been seen on this machine. But it wasn't mowing that I wanted anyway. I wanted something to ride—something with an engine, something without pedals.

At age 12, I was forbidden by my parents to have a mini-bike, a go-kart or a three-wheeler (for those under 30, that's a prehistoric four-wheeler). However, when I traded my neighbor Terry two push mowers and $5 in cash for this odd machine, my parents finally relented. Of course, the mower topped out at a whopping 3 or 4 miles per hour. While I wasn't exactly off to the races, it was better than the alternative: my Schwinn 5-speed bicycle (with pedals and no engine).

Things were looking up. One day soon after the purchase, Terry, whose dad owned a small-engine repair shop, had a brainstorm. He wanted to rework the belts on the bottom of my machine to see if it would go faster. He warned me that even if it worked, the belts would wear out quickly. So what's a few extra bucks when there's a need for speed? He tried; it did work.

Immediately, I moved into the realm of double-digit racing—kickin' up dust at a blistering 12 to 13 mph. I got so inspired that I painted my baby blue, boldly scribbling the name Blue Bonnet Racer across the side. I know, an ironic title for a lad growing up in the midst of engineless Amish country. But things like that don't have to make sense. It felt good, and we went everywhere together.

Living as we did on a small farm just outside a small and rural Indiana town, I drove the Blue Bonnet all over the countryside, down by the railroad tracks and to the store to buy milk and bread when Mom sent me.

The Blue Bonnet proved to be more than just a luxury. I put it to work. Using some rope, twine and a couple of bungee cords from the barn, I managed to mount our wheelbarrow on the back to resemble a miniature

dump truck. It was great for hauling grass clippings, leaves, and potatoes and corn from the garden. I actually enjoyed chores now.

With the Blue Bonnet at my disposal, it seemed everything was more fun. To paraphrase the old ad jingle: Everything was better with Blue Bonnet on it, or at least the Blue Bonnet was better with me on it. And anything was possible—well, almost anything. I did have one experiment that was less than a resounding success...

In fact, the only time Ol' Blue didn't come through was when I tried to use it for its original purpose: mowing. We had three acres of lawn to attend to, and when the family lawn and garden tractor broke down, the alternative was the illustrious push mower. (Yes, we still had one left.) And I do mean push. I don't think they made self-propelled mowers in 1977. At least not where I lived. Anyhow, my mind was working overtime so that my arms and legs wouldn't have to.

That's it! Mount the push mower on the back of the Blue Bonnet. I returned to the barn and got out the rope, twine and bungees that worked so well with the wheelbarrow. No dice. It cut the grass all right, but not in straight rows. That thing was zigzagging everywhere.

Ultimately, I had to give the "racer" a break while I paid my "farm boy" dues.

That's okay. Blue Bonnet and I were back in action the next day. Well, you've heard it said, "When life tosses you lemons, make lemonade"—nothing new there. But I say, "When life sends you a mower, make a racer."

It just goes to show that sometimes in the goofy antics of a child are found life-changing questions, such as: "What are you sitting on? And how fast are you going?"

FRESH FROM THE FARM

The summer I was 10 years old, my parents moved my two brothers and me from our suburban mainstay to a small farm complete with barn, chicken house and even some fruit trees and grape vines. The old neighborhood had plenty of character, and characters, and there was always something to do. As a result, I felt less than pleased about the move.

Little did I know, a whole new world awaited… Although the new homestead sat officially in the "boonies," we weren't completely desolate. Our property sat on the first lot outside the city limits—which put us a couple stone throws from a small, Amish town called Millersburg.

Most of the people living in and around the town carried the last name of Miller. Well, that is except for many with the last name of Yoder. As a child, I always wondered how many Yoders short we were of being the town of Yodersburg. It couldn't have been that many, in fact, I'm surprised they had not asked for a recount.

The town of 800 demonstrated some colloquial charm with two grain mills, a gas station, a quaint country store and a restaurant my brothers and I were warned to stay away from—Margie's Lounge. Margie's was the only thing ever open past 6 o'clock in that town.

Adjusting to the town had little bearing on my family though. It was country living that perplexed the parents. It's important to note at this point that Mom and Dad had both grown up in good-sized towns before moving to the 'burbs. They knew nothing of farm life, but for some reason, they were determined to dig in and try to become country folk.

The first summer and fall on the farm offered some excitement and a few changes as Mom, normally known by those near her as an outstanding cook, altered her usual approach. I'm not sure her status changed completely, but wholesome eating became the charge from the kitchen. When Mom did bake some goodies

like cookies or cake, things looked a little darker and different as white flour had been replaced by wheat flour, wheat germ and anything else wheatie that could be considered healthy.

If we found that hard to swallow (and let's face it, the cookies weren't disappearing at the usual rapid rate), Mom had a healthy beverage to wash it down with. Yes, our own homemade grape juice. Just a few days (day and night) of labor produced a two-year supply of this illustrious liquid. Some jars were light blue, some dark blue and still some even purple.

Each glass offered an adventure. As long as you were careful of the skins that somehow made it through the strainer, it was fairly tasty.

Finally, what farm is complete without a garden? My Mother confessed that she had dreamed of having her own garden and Dad was quick to jump aboard the project. With plenty of land behind the barn, and three healthy boys at their beck and call, why not? Seeds were purchased, and the planting began—planting and more planting. By the time we finished, we had a patch as large as a football field.

That was the easy part. Maintaining offered more of a challenge. Despite the family's determination, reality set in and much of the garden (from the 20-

yard line all the way to the goal posts) turned to weeds. However, we didn't punt completely. A proud crop was harvested, and we enjoyed corn, lettuce, tomatoes and even potatoes in the fall.

Fall also brought the last of the year's events that I recall and what an oddity…

It all started with the town of Millersburg wanting to hook us and our neighbors to their new sewer system. Sure, a portion of our property was a big pile of mud, but that offered little inconvenience so all was well—we thought. One evening, our neighbor, Gary, was enjoying the latest edition of *Field and Stream* from atop the family throne (toilet) when suddenly, he heard a strange splashing in the bowl below him. Before he could investigate, a large sewer rat jumped out between his legs and scampered for the living room.

While pulling up his trousers, Gary, being a long-time hunter, grabbed knife and bow and arrow and chased the critter into the basement. There the expedition quickly ended with Gary emerging as the victor.

Upon hearing of the previous night's activity, my folks were not taking this lying down. However, we had no gun, bow and arrow or even knife (well, with the exception of a steak knife that is), so prevention became the call of the wild (sorry, I couldn't resist that one).

The plan: place heavy barbells atop each of the two toilet seats and, of course, remove all reading materials as to do your "business" and move on. Why the barbells? Simple, if a sewer rat makes it through, at least trap the varmint. No reason to give it free passage.

That's quite a lot of activity for a first year in a new home. Originally, my parents moved us to the country to better our lives. I guess there's no way of knowing if it was better than the 'burbs; however, I did emerge with a few wacky stories and an even wackier family.

SUMMER OF REGRET AND THE FIST I MET

I remember well the summer I was 13 years old. Even though it was many years ago, I remember it because I did nothing—nothing useful anyway. The thought of that wasted time still haunts me, motivates me to never forget the preciousness of a single day, especially a summer day. It was the last summer of my life I would not be required to have a steady job. Instead, I spent it sitting around Greg Juday's house. Greg lived in town just a short bike ride from my country home and although he was a year younger than me, we got along okay. The draw to spend time with Greg was not so much a buddy-buddy relationship; it had more to do with the fact that his parents were not home during the day. I guess there was sort of a freedom there. Yet every day I left for his house, I felt like a part of me was dying.

It's not that we did anything wrong. We watched TV, sat around inside and out, and sometimes even ran around the house itself. It was pointless.

Interestingly enough, there was one major event that did take place there right before summer would end, launch us into a new grade in school, and cure me of the Greg Juday blues forever.

Greg and I were sitting on the porch killing time, per usual, one afternoon when Mike, a younger and much rougher character, came walking toward Greg's house. I didn't think much of it at first since Mike dropped by from time to time to share a few new cuss words or phrases he had learned from his even shadier older brother. Only this time, somebody was following Mike—somebody gigantic whom we'd never seen before.

He and Mike made themselves at home on Greg's porch. We were told that "Ricky" was Mike's 15-year-old cousin from the city. He was from a much larger town, he was much larger, and he told tales that were larger yet.

For the next few days, Mike and Ricky seemed to stop by Greg's porch more and more with exaggerated stories of Ricky's greatness. We were told that Ricky was a karate "black belt" as well as a dirt bike champion and the yarn did spin and spin.

Finally, I could take it no more. Greg and I got on the phone one afternoon and called up Mike's house and asked for Ricky. When he answered, all I wanted to say for days just poured out: "Hey Ricky, I'd sure like to see those trophies, Vrrrm Vrrrm! You couldn't stay on a bike, let alone race one. You big, fat liar!"

And the insults kept coming until I finally hung up, and Greg and I laughed uncontrollably. That was the most fun I had there all summer until we looked across the street and saw Ricky and Mike coming in a huff.

Greg quickly locked the door in the kitchen and we continued to laugh as the two boys approached. I couldn't resist from tossing a few more insults as Ricky glared at me through the screen door.

Ricky pounded the door a few times and then made a threat to Greg, "You better open this door before I break it down."

I just chuckled all the more until Greg walked directly over and unlocked the door. To this day, I have no idea what he was thinking. I froze with my mouth wide

open. Finally, I came to my senses, but it was too late—there was no place to run. I walked into the dining room with Ricky right on my heels. He didn't say anything. He just handed his cigarette to Mike, stepped up to me and punched me in the face four or five times. He retrieved his cigarette and calmly walked out of the house. I stood there in shock for a moment, then ran to my bike and peddled away, never to return to Greg's house again.

I went home but told nobody what had happened. It was like a dream. I could see him hitting my face, but I didn't feel anything (well, at least until the next morning). But I didn't care — I was alive again.

I got knocked right out of that stupor I had been in most of the summer, and I wasn't sorry. I wasn't sorry it happened, and I wasn't sorry for what I had said to Ricky. It was the truth. The only regret I had was this had happened in the last few weeks of summer instead of the first.

It's funny. The pain from those punches lasted a few days, but the bitterness from those wasted summer days still sits in a corner of my soul. And I'm glad, because never again will I take for granted the summer sun, imagination or youth.

TROUBLE WITH THE TOWNIES

The summer I was to be in fifth grade, my parents moved us to a small farm just outside the tiny, little town called Millersburg, Indiana. My father was a teacher and coach at the local high school there, and he wanted his boys to be near him. So we packed up and left our suburban paradise and moved just 15 miles south.

Sure, it was a nice piece of property with a barn, a chicken house and plenty of room to roam. But it wasn't what we gained that bothered me so much as what we left behind: my first love, friends to fight for and friends who would fill a baseball field in five minutes flat.

My Dad assured me friends could be found anywhere and so I headed to the nearby town to discover the wisdom of his words. He was often right, but unfortunately in this case, reality would prove otherwise.

I was a confident athlete since my father was a coach, and we had played sports often in the old 'hood. So when I went to town, it was in hopes of finding a friendly game of anything. Sure enough, I found some games of football and basketball. But when I joined in, I heard insults. Two kids in particular (Darrel and Steve) scowled and whenever they got a chance, hit me extra hard or took cheap shots.

I just didn't like the "townies." To me, all of them seemed rough and rude and ready to hurt anyone at a moment's notice just because they could. I stopped trying to fit in and avoided town except for Little League baseball, of course. As maybe a little poetic justice, my team won the Little League championship both my elementary years.

Soon, school started, and I made many friends, most of whom were like me and lived outside of town. But when school ended for the summer, my friends were way out on the farm and I was stuck with the townies.

That is, until Brett moved in. He had a motorcycle, an easy-go-lucky personality and the townies left him alone—more importantly, they left me alone when I was with him.

Brett was nice and had the "cool" thing going for him, but as I would soon discover, Brett was a little on the "wild" side as well. I'll never forget one day when he and I were hanging around his house (his parents were seldom home) and a kid named Brian Sideler stopped by on his little motorcycle. The two of them instantly lit up a cigarette together right there in the front yard. I was shocked. Well, by Brett, not by Brian.

I had already heard that Brian was a self-proclaimed devil worshiper and possibly a drug user too at the tender age of 12. I don't know if it was true, but he sure looked the part and I had never even spoken to him.

Funny thing, while the two of them were enjoying their summertime smoke, I got inspired. I don't know exactly what it was. I got mad; I got adventurous; I got on Brian's little Kawasaki 75 and I took off like the dickens toward the trails behind the new houses just being built. Both boys were startled and then Brian hopped on Brett's Kawasaki 100 and started chasing me.

He didn't catch me. I rode like a crazy man on a mission. He gave up. I rode the trails for a while and

then I circled back and pulled into Brett's driveway. I instantly got off the motorbike and stood face-to-face with the two boys. Neither one of them did anything so I got on my Schwinn 5-speed bike and rode away. As I peddled out of the driveway, Brett called to me and said, "Man, what did you do that for?" I just kept on riding. I never went back to his house again.

When I saw Brett at school or in town, he was always pleasant and friendly to me but whatever friendship we had ended that day. It wasn't because of my trip on the trails. Those guys were headed for trouble. It just clicked in me that day: their actions didn't line up with who I was or who I wanted to be.

I started to settle into my new surroundings and by junior high, townies were not an issue to me; however, I do remember one last situation with a "townie." Interestingly enough, it took place in Phys. Ed where we had been paired with boys our size during a unit on wrestling.

I did not like to fight, wrestle or any of that stuff, but in this case, I had no choice. I had been paired with Steve Morton. The fact that he ran with the tough townie bunch is about all I knew of him. I assumed he must be versed in the art of fight, and I was concerned my clock was about to be cleaned.

So I watched others wrestle and worked out a strategy in preparation for our Monday morning match. I was so emotionally wired by the time we hit the mat, you would have thought I was a linebacker for the Chicago Bears.

As soon as the whistle blew, I tackled Steve at the knees, knocked him to the ground and jumped on top of him. I pinned him in a gym class record of nine seconds. Poor Steve, who obviously didn't want to wrestle any more than I did, laid there stunned.

Shoot, some of the townies just like some of the farm boys, turned out to be fine young men and some didn't. It's so easy to develop an "us against them" mentality.

Even when I reflect on those times, I still feel an anger burning against those boys. But why? I had my share of victories. No matter. I was intimidated by them and perhaps they by me. Come to find out, none of us ever emerge the victor when we're not at peace with ourselves.

TWO POINTS FOR STAYING OUT OF TROUBLE

It was the last day of school. Paul and I could sit tight no more. With just one hour left, we exited the library, leaving many of our freshman friends behind.

Paul slipped down to his locker to get his basketball, and I met him at the gym lobby. Perfect. The gym sat dark and desolate as I finagled my comb to open the lightly secured door. I had done this trick many times in the morning when I headed to school early with my Dad, who was a teacher, but never had I attempted this trick during school hours.

We got into the gym safe and sound. As always, there were two, tiny safety bulbs casting just enough light to see one of the baskets and the foul line. It was a glorious glow for me. I had been there many times, but it took a little getting used to for Paul.

Before long, we were laughing, playing, shooting and shouting as summer was but a bell away. But wait! We heard the squeaking of the gym door at the corner of the facility, just on the other side of the folded bleachers. Somebody was coming.

Paul and I dove under some open bleachers just a few feet from the basket. Heels clicked and clamored on the wood flooring as they moved closer to us. We were cooked, or so I thought. But wait. I could see a group of people at the end of the court. Their voices echoed across the dark gym. I recognized the principal and Superintendent Bose. I had caddied for him at many a golf outing with my Dad. There also were a few other men in suits and ties pointing and talking. They continued their conversation for a few moments, then turned and left. Paul and I dared not to move—or even breathe. After a minute or so, we crawled out from under the bleachers.

"You don't suppose…" Paul said. Suddenly a smile brushed across his face. "They didn't hear us!"

We leaped into the air for a high-five. I fired up a hook shot, and Paul retrieved with passion. He drove

toward me and put in a fancy, double-pump layup, and I whopped him on the head.

Squeak! The corner door opened again. Immediately we heard, "You go this way, and I'll go around. They may still be here."

Paul and I ran toward the other side of the bleachers. There lay an old wrestling mat rolled up in the darkness, and we quickly crawled inside. Within a few seconds I heard one of the Phys. Ed teachers yell, "They're not over here!"

She couldn't have been more than five feet from my trembling hands. After she had gone around the corner and left the gym, we wiggled out of the mats and headed for the exit. As soon as we hit the doors, sunshine flooded the gymnasium, and the doors slammed shut. Obviously, it wasn't Elvis who had just left the building.

Paul and I were jogging around outside and didn't know what to do. Even though we were quite sure the school officials didn't know who the culprits were, we were in trouble since there was still a half hour left before the bell – and the buses wouldn't roll in for some time. We knew that if we got caught outside the building it would be an even bigger offense than sneaking into the gym. We had no choice: We had to get back into the school.

Fortunately, there was a lot of traffic by the Industrial Arts Center, and we slipped right in among a number of students. Paul and I split up, hoping one of us would make it to the summer crime-free, at least uncharged anyway.

He headed for the west restroom and I, the east. Just as I locked the door in the back stall, I heard over the P.A. system, "Would Troy Kidder please report to the office?" What?! How did they know it was me? Not two minutes later, my Dad walked in, came directly to the last stall and called out, "Son, they want you at the office. You'd better get going." So I did.

As I walked into the principal's office, there was Paul sitting directly in front of Mr. Bose. Paul didn't look pleased; neither did Mr. Bose.

It seems Paul never made it to his last stall and was nabbed upon entrance. Before we could compare notes any further, we were sentenced (but the punishment wasn't enough to cause much remorse for me or Paul).

However, I was baffled. How did they know it was me in the dark gym? And how did my Dad know to look in the last stall in the east restroom?

Well, I learned that even when we think we're doing something unusually sneaky, often the only one we're really fooling is ourselves.

THE THREE BALL CHALLENGE

Sink 19 in their face!

As some may relate, those early high school years were awkward and difficult for me. Although not my only interest, I hid myself in sports. My father had been a great college athlete (and now a coach at the same school I attended) and my older brother was an outstanding basketball player in his own right.

Sure, it was instant respect and acceptance in some circles coming from a basketball family in the heart of the Hoosier state, but jealousy, resentment and other pressures seemed to ride on the same back as the good.

I remember especially my sophomore year. My brother was a senior and one of the country's leading scorers, and I was starting to do okay myself. In all honesty, the recognition I received — congratulations from the elder fans and a few photos in the local paper — was still more on name than merit, but I felt good.

That settling in never did run its course to the boo birds, jealous classmates and believe it or not, sarcastic teachers, who made comments in class such as, "is this really the next great Kidder in our midst?" It made school full of tension for me, and I seldom felt that I could let my guard down.

I recall one lunch hour in particular. I was sitting with some friends, enjoying a chocolate shake (our high school made great shakes), when a senior boy, not an athlete, came up to me and began harassing me. He wanted the whole table to know, if not the entire cafeteria, that in his opinion, I was "not that good of a shooter."

My friends told him to "shut up" but he continued on and finally challenged me to go into the gym with him on a milkshake bet that I couldn't make just three shots in a row from atop the key. (That's the circle

4-feet beyond the free-throw line.) I accepted, and off we went. By the time we arrived in the gym, there were 15 or 20 onlookers discussing their own view of what I could do.

In reality, my confidence was high, having grown up on this court and played during all hours of the day and night.

I quickly sank the three. Dejected, the challenger put his head down and mumbled, "Let's go get your shake."

Sure, I won the bet, but it didn't feel over to me. There was still an anger burning in my gut. Tomorrow it could be someone else with the same challenge telling me I was lucky the day before. No, I had to remove all doubt. "Wait," I said. "Give me the ball!"

I continued to sink 19 in a row before finally missing. By now, I had won over a few doubters in the crowd, and I walked off the court to several pats on the back.

But before you think this is just some old guy reliving the "glory days," think again. Yes, I'm proud of the way I rose to the occasion, but the lesson lives on. If we're going to do anything worthwhile in life, there's always going to be the boo birds, the jealous peers and the sarcastic superiors. For some reason, they're just a little more difficult to spot now that we're older.

Next time you rise to the occasion and stir an enemy to a three-ball challenge, sink 19 in their face and make everyone count in the spirit of a skinny Hoosier boy. After all, life is grand for those who dare take a shot while others sit comfortably in the stands with popcorn in hand and criticize.

THANK YOU, MRS. CRISMAN

Although my Dad would become my high school basketball coach upon entering my eighth-grade year in school, he felt it inappropriate for me to have him as a teacher. I was bumped to the "other" History teacher's class, Mrs. Crisman. She was new to our school and unknown to us at the time. I am truly thankful that she made an appearance when she did. It was a good experience.

Short and thick and about 50 years old, nothing really drew me to her at first, but time and attention changed that. The first thing I noticed about her was that I was not judged base on who my Dad was. I started at scratch—what a nice change. The other teachers acted like they knew me, since they knew my Dad, and I got treated accordingly. Whether they liked him or not, some kind of baggage got dragged into the relationship.

I could feel that in every class, and quite honestly, I resented it greatly. Like all unique characters, Mrs. Crisman had her oddities (or in this case, maybe vices). For example, all the students knew that she smoked several cigarettes per day. The gray cloud that surrounded her gave that away. In fact, her classroom often reeked of the stuff. And when I dared scamper to her desk to ask a question, she always had Hall's (extra, hefty menthol) cough drops in her mouth. Perhaps she thought it hid the tobacco smell, or maybe she just enjoyed them.

There were also rumors of the excessive use of hard liquor, although I don't know how anyone could have known for sure. And on occasion, she had let a few "bad" words slip out during time of instruction, anger and even merriment.

Regardless of all these things, she was my favorite teacher. Although she ruled her classroom with a strong arm of authority, I know that she had a delightful sense of humor.

I recall one particular situation in which the entire class was waiting for the end of the day announcements

as we always did in her class. They didn't come on. Finally, I cupped my hands around my nose and loudly declared, "No announcements today; students are dismissed."

This was not meant as an act of deception, but merely a joke. However, I must have done a good job, and considering that my seat was located directly below the speaker, I sent all students packing and out the door. Mrs. Crisman smiled and said goodbye like any other day. My buddy, Greg Hite, and I sat there in amazement as the students continued to file out.

Just as the entire class hit the hallway, the "real" announcements came over the speaker system. Mrs. Crisman looked at Greg and I and leaped from behind her desk to usher each student back into the classroom.

She looked my way, noticing that we had stayed while everyone else left. Greg blurted out, "It was Troy. It was Troy. He fooled you all!" Nobody dared to say a word, waiting for Mrs. Crisman's response: She cracked a smile and busted out laughing and the entire class joined in. Nobody heard announcements the day.

And finally, I remember the time we had an end of the semester test. It was to be an open note test since most eighth-graders seldom take notes or hold onto old assignments. But for some reason, I had a whole folder of notes and I did very well. In fact, I was the only one in the class able to fill in all the United States on the blank map.

She was so proud of me. She even told my Dad and he, being a history teacher, was proud too. Mrs. Crisman never did ask me if I filled in the map by memory or if I had held onto the assignment that we did early in the year. She assumed it was by memory and I never did tell anyone the entire story. Come to think of it, she would have been proud either way.

It just goes to show that when it all comes down, it's not so much the oddities or even the vices that we remember about folks, it's how we were treated. That makes all the difference. Thanks, Mrs. Crisman.

THE SOUL OF A BOY

PITCH, PLEASE—BUT NO ANTS ALLOWED

In the summer of '75, I was about to enter sixth grade, but first it was fastballs in the summer Little League. I pitched my team to a championship that summer, and then it was off to Millersburg Elementary for my final year of grammar school.

The year went well, and I was up to my old tricks as the perennial prankster, always looking to see just how far I could push without getting pushed back too hard. I literally ran a pair of Fruit of the Looms up the flagpole one morning (size 42s, believe it or not). Greg Hite and I had found them in the school "Lost and Found" box. Even with my overactive imagination, I had no idea how they got in there.

Greg and I also threw some lighted firecrackers into the school auditorium, hid Mr. Ritchie's chair on a regular basis, and just plain disturbed the educational process whenever possible.

I remember as I was walking into Mrs. Weybright's class one morning, she looked at me from across the room and loudly proclaimed, "I'm not in the mood for that today. To the office!" I was stunned. I hadn't even said a word.

But she was a woman of rare discernment. Finally, school ended, and I passed with a one-way ticket to junior high (bad grades or good, I was sure I wouldn't be invited to stay another year). In the summer, it was back to my first love, baseball. This would be my last year in Little League, and I wanted to leave a legacy: repeat as champions.

Being a year older, I pitched even better. In fact, in one game I struck out every batter I faced. But before you start thinking this is some professional athlete looking back at his "humble" beginnings, let me assure you that this isn't the case. Sure, we went on to win the title again, but I would have one more memorable moment on the baseball diamond.

Not only did we win the championship that summer, I grew up as well. I put away those childish pranks (for the most part) as I headed into junior high with a new

attitude. Maybe, just maybe, some of that change had to do with the fact that my Dad was a teacher and coach at the junior high where I was to attend. Whatever stunt I pulled at school was sure to get punished double at home.

I finished seventh grade with new friends and grades that would make any Mom proud. As summer baseball began, it became obvious that, as a seventh-grader on a seventh- and eighth-grade team, I wouldn't dominate like Little League. The older boys seemed to smack my fast one around with ease.

That might have bothered me the year before, but with my new attitude and good grades it didn't mean that much. I felt good about myself. I was even reading books in the summer now. It was while reading a book that I came across a word, a word I would soon get to tryout… on the ball diamond.

The book was an old science manual that my Mom had purchased at the garage sale. The word was "pissant," meaning an ant noted for the order of its formic acid. Even though I had turned over a proverbial new leaf, I was still a kid — a kid who liked to shock folks on occasion. This seemed like the perfect word for doing that. It sounded naughty, but it couldn't be that bad; it was real bug. The science book said so. I began looking for the opportune moment. One day during baseball practice, the moment came.

While sitting in the dugout awaiting my turn at bat, Darrel Troyer, one of our best players, got a hit and began racing for first but, for no apparent reason, tripped and hit the ground hard. The stage was set. All eyes were on Darrel. Nobody moved. Right on cue, I yelled, "What's the matter, Darrel? Trip on a pissant?"

The other boys erupted with laughter, until my Dad yelled back at me, "What did you say?"

I knew well enough he had heard it, and that wisdom would suggest not actually repeating it.

"You hit the showers, Troy. You're done for the day." Funny enough, Dad never mentioned it again, but I did. Just the other day (about 25 years later) my family and I were at a restaurant with my parents. For some reason I remembered this story and told my Dad the whole thing. He laughed and laughed, confessing he had no recollection of it at all.

It just goes to show that not only does time heal wounds, it puts passionate moments in perspective. And all of us must admit that at one time or another — especially as parents — we must have made a mountain out of a molehill or, in this case, an anthill.

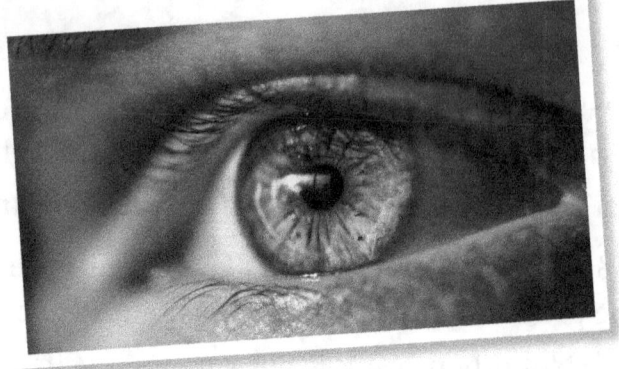

JACK AN EYE

Isn't it funny how things stick to the soul and don't want to let go? I was shooting some hoops the other day and for some reason my mind replayed an incident from the summer of my freshman year in high school some 25 years earlier.

I was 15 years old and had set a goal to improve in my basketball skills by practicing every day and by going away to basketball camp at a college just 30 miles away. I had exceeded all hopes the prior season by being moved up from the freshmen team to play at the junior varsity level, and I even got invited to practice with the varsity squad on occasion. My sophomore year was to be my "break out" year and I just knew this week-long camp would help me develop the edge I needed.

The first two days went well. I worked hard, met new friends, and began to establish myself as one to be watched. However, things were about to change. That night as I headed across the lobby to the cola machines, I passed most of the campers and counselors huddled around the television to watch the baseball all-star game. Not interested in the game, I walked away, minding my own business, directly to the vending machines. One of the counselors (Kent) yelled out, "Hey Kidder! Get over here. I need a back rub."

Having already been warned that the counselors often treated the kids as their personal lackies, I was ready. Besides, he already had two campers attending to his needs. Without further thought, I proclaimed, "I didn't come here to rub your back. I came to play basketball." I continued on my way.

Now that the entire camp was watching, he couldn't let it ride. He jumped to his feet and got right in my face and said, "What did you say?"

A little intimidated by his towering height and large biceps, I meekly repeated, "I'm here to play ball, not rub your back." He said, "We'll see about that," as he grabbed my arm.

Just then, a strange resolve came over me. I yanked my arm away and said, "Yes, we will see. I'm going to ask

the coach if I have to rub your back." Kent consented, and I quickly headed down the hallway toward the coach's office while the campers quieted, waiting to see how this might end.

I knocked on the coach's door and he quickly invited me in. To my surprise, he had apparently just gotten out of the shower. He sported a t-shirt, sweat pants and was toweling off his hair while talking on the phone. I tried to exit quickly, but he encouraged me to tell him what the trouble seemed to be. I gave him the synopsis and his answer was startling to say the least: "Tell him to Jack an Eye!"

"What?"

He reiterated, "You don't have to rub his back. Tell him to Jack an Eye.

"Thank you, Coach," I squeaked out on my way back to the boys. I was about to use a phrase that I'd heard neither before or since. It sure sounded provocative, maybe even a little vulgar. I couldn't wait to use it.

As I entered the lobby, everyone was waiting for the verdict. With each step my confidence grew and grew. Finally, without missing a beat I looked the counselor in the eyes and blurted out: "Jack an Eye."

Chins hit the floor and Kent jumped up and literally ran to cut me off. So I repeated myself, "The coach told me to tell you to 'Jack an Eye.' Go ask him," I added. Then I walked out of the lobby, leaving a rather stunned group of campers and counselors behind.

Needless to say, the rest of my camp experience was tension filled. The counselors who refereed our games let people foul me without a call and in turn, called fouls on me I never committed. The other kids stayed clear of me for obvious reasons and at 15, this was tough to take emotionally.

Admittedly, I went to bed a couple of nights with a few tears in my eyes, but somehow managed to turn in the best performance of my basketball life as I led my team in scoring and to the championship. I also made it to the finals in two individual competitions. But to nobody's surprise, my name did not appear on the all-star roster.

Sadly, what should have been at least a moment of joy and accomplishment for a young boy ended only in a burning sense of injustice. I'm willing to bet that you too have a few of those lodged in your gut as well — a moment of triumph ruined by poor leadership or abuse of power.

But before we curse everyone that ever hurt us, let's make that burn count. Let's make a decree that we will not abuse our power, our realm of authority.

Every day we have an opportunity to knock someone down or build them up. So when things get tough, let's forget about the "Jack an Eye," an "Eye for an Eye," and remember, "The greatest of these is love."

TROY KIDDER

THE GIANT OVERPASS

I grew up in a small, Indiana farm town. With approximately 800 people in the city limits. Our commerce boasted a grocery store, two gas stations, a hardware store, a feed mill and oh yes, one giant overpass.

Since the railroad tracks, at one time, ran across the very entrance of this so-called city, the wisdom of the elders some 50 years prior had built a large overpass (also known as "The Bridge") for people to enter the city limits without disturbance or delay and in hopes of speeding growth. It seems the idea was a great success as Millersburg, Indiana, grew another 200 to 300 people over the next half century.

Okay, so maybe it didn't payoff quite like they had hoped. However, it sure meant a lot to me as a child since my parents bought a small farm barely a quarter mile from the bridge itself on the outskirts of town. There was but one other entrance, but most used the illustrious overpass. As a result, if anything happened in town, or was going to happen, it passed by us first. I felt like I had a finger on the pulse of activity. A powerful feeling for a 10-year-old boy with nothing else to do all summer but ride mini-bikes and shoot baskets at the barn.

Believe it or not, a lot did happen. Maybe not great things by some standards, but events that I remember, events that shape our lives. For example, I remember late one night while in bed, I heard the sporadic clip-clop-clip-clop of a horse running out of control. Its Amish passenger in the buggy was yelling, "Woah, Woah!" at the top of his lungs.

By the time I got out of bed, I could see him racing toward the overpass. It scared me since once you started over the bridge, you must take a quick left into town or a quick right out of town. Those who missed would take a quick ride down a grassy hill and smack right into the hardware store's storage barn. Fortunately, that didn't happen.

Even scarier was the time two huge semi-trucks got stuck on the overpass at the same time. Having been built in the 1930s, this bridge had an iron top and these trailers stood tall and caught the top of our bridge. I watched in anxious anticipation as I could imagine the trucks and bridge crashing to the railroad tracks beneath. There was banging, clanging, cussing and praying for about three or four hours before finally working the trucks free.

And, of course, I remember the time my neighbor, Ricky, was throwing rocks down at the train as it passed below. He reached down and pulled a hunk of cement from the bridge itself (it was shedding a lot in those later days) and he grunted in effort as he could barely hoist it over the rail. Finally, it dropped as if in slow motion. We watched as the mammoth rock headed directly for the railroad car full of autos.

These weren't just any vehicles, but the AMC Pacer—not only the ugliest car ever made, but the one with the largest back window. I'll never forget the explosion that rear window made upon impact with the hunk of cement. It was as if it had been blown out with a bomb.

Call it ill timing or the toss of a lifetime, but it happened. We both watched in disbelief. A numbing feeling came over my legs and I couldn't move. I knew

that I should run or something, but I couldn't. When I got back my senses, I told Ricky that was about the dumbest thing I ever saw anybody do. He didn't argue, and we scarcely mentioned it again.

By the time I entered junior high, our illustrious bridge was condemned and finally closed, a modern bridge built in its place. It was perfect timing as my world was expanding and that old bridge didn't mean much anymore.

But for a time, it meant everything. Sometimes, it's just enjoyable to remember…

TROY KIDDER

BAREFOOT ON A BANANA

I met the twins, Ron and Richard Carpenter, in fifth grade just after I moved to the small farm town of Millersburg, Indiana. As I had many new friends to meet, I didn't really notice them that much until Ron got his leg caught in an auger at the family-owned grain mill.

I remember seeing a picture of Ron in the paper and reading a quote from him saying "thank you" after the firefighters rescued him.

A few months later, Ron returned to school with a wooden leg and received the compassion of his classmates. But it wasn't long before Ron's fun-loving personality won the hearts of his fellow students, and

the grace of our compassion was no longer needed. Ron was one of us again.

By the time junior high rolled around, my parents had switched churches, and I was attending the same one as "the boys," as I had begun to call them. I got to know them better as we now did things together at both school and church.

Ron had a quick wit and a good set shot, and Richard would smile from ear to ear, reminiscent of Milton Berle. Richard also liked girls. Not in a provocative sense, but in appreciation. He would watch them and joke with them. He had a gentleness about him that would be even more rare these days, and the girls seemed to enjoy him. But Richard was shy and graduated from high school without ever asking a girl on a date.

At church, Mr. Carpenter, the boys' dad, was our Sunday School teacher. He was older than my parents, yet full of life. He was a parental prankster who would tease the girls and hassle the guys, and we all loved it. The church parties at the Carpenters' place were like no other. There were hayrides at their farm, and in the barn we would walk barefoot in the dark, stepping on items that we were told were edible. Have you ever stepped on a banana in your bare feet?

Mrs. Carpenter was one for details, and she loved to serve others. I remember dinner at their place one evening. She stood in the kitchen, apron tied around her waist, with sleeves rolled up, refusing to eat until everyone else was happily fed. I don't know of a time when I was visiting that some form of goodies wasn't baking in her oven.

The boys' older sister, Deb, was an attractive young lady and, like her mother, an outstanding cook. Deb had spunk, and we liked to see her temper flare. We would hide her stuff and call her to the phone when nobody was there — anything to get her goat. Most of our pranks worked, and all in all, I think she probably enjoyed some of them too.

I spent more and more time with the Carpenters, and the boys and I went to high school together as well. They were good students and very respectful of their elders, which makes what happened in our accounting class even funnier.

We had a teacher named Mrs. Hughes. We liked to joke with her before and after class when we felt she would appreciate it. One day before class, Ron, Richard and I had a question and headed to her office, which was situated directly behind her classroom. After surveying the office, and finding her absent, Ron saw a

large broom in the corner and quipped, "She couldn't have gone too far; her broom is still here."

Mrs. Hughes, it turned out, had been standing directly behind us and surprised us all with the comment, "So I'm a witch, am I?"

Ron's mouth dropped wide open and he turned beet red. We awkwardly walked away with no mention of it again from Mrs. Hughes, though I thought I heard her chuckling as we made our retreat. She knew Ron well enough to know that no punishment could ever accomplish what he already felt when he saw her face.

Ron went on to take more classes from Mrs. Hughes and credited her in part for his present career as an accountant. Richard went back to college 10 years after high school, I'm told, and is now preparing to answer a call to the ministry.

As I remember these special folks, I realize that their openness in both triumph and adversity was a form of humility that allowed others in.

I'm beginning to understand that there is no greater opportunity in life than relationships. I count myself truly blessed for having known the Carpenter family.

TROY KIDDER

THE JELL-O® AND AUNT JOSIE

Like most, when I think of Thanksgiving, I picture turkey and pies and Jell-O® desserts of various shapes and sizes sitting tightly on every corner of the table. I remember my relatives of various shapes and sizes crammed into one living room, the folks every bit resembling the food on our table.

I recall Aunt Josie and Aunt May wanting to hug my little 7-year-old body as soon as I walked in the door. My brother Todd was the shrewd one. He would run around until they finally gave up. I was the loving, sensitive one who hated to see an older lady out of breath from a chase.

Soon, however, it would be me out of breath from one of their mammoth hugs. Both ladies were heavyset

with ample bosoms and manly grips. Aunt Josie especially would get a hold of me and shove my face directly into her nurturing zone where air was hard to find. I would soon be pounding her back — an act she perceived as affection but was really a plea for release.

My uncles were not quite as playful, and seldom did I exchange much dialog with any of them. There was my Uncle Jerry and, although he said very little, I liked him. I think it's because he always had this smirk on his face that made me wonder what put it there. But when you're seven, you ponder these things, and you don't ask because you're liable to get your face slapped.

That's another thing about these "get-togethers." After the food is consumed, the adults get crabby and the slightest disturbance brings a strong reprimand. I noticed that my uncles seldom yelled at their own kids but went right for the nephews. My Dad, however, was the only one who was impartial. He would yell equally at my brother, me and our cousins without prejudice.

We as kids, believe it or not, weren't bothered by all the post-meal crankiness. We loved what followed. For example, Great-Grandma Mahoney would be sitting on the chair talking and, one minute later, she was sound asleep. She could wake up after a five-minute snooze and pick up right where she left off ... amazing.

But what we really loved was the after-dinner card playing. If there's one thing kids love, it's watching adults get irritable with each other. My uncles could sit in a room with a group of people for hours and not say two words, but as soon as the Rook cards were on the tables they would be spittin' and sputterin' like old ladies at a tea party.

Aunt Josie and Uncle Harold were the funniest, though. They always had to play on the same team. They wouldn't hear of it any other way. Then they fought through every hand. It didn't matter what Harold did, it was always a "bonehead play," according to Aunt Josie. Finally, when Uncle Harold had had enough, he would get brave and tell his wife to "pipe down." That actually worked for a few moments, but then it was back to the barking.

Occasionally, we would interrupt Aunt Josie to ask her a question or offer her a cookie while she was scowling at her husband. She would look over at us, and immediately her face melted to her sweetness with a "yes, dear." If Uncle Harold had been clever at all, he would have paid us a buck to interrupt frequently. I suppose it wouldn't have mattered much since it took

Aunt Josie only a turn of the neck to revert to form. I'm not sure about this, but I always thought Uncle Harold heard it all the way home too. A price to be paid for a passionate woman.

Most of my cousins were girls and, as a result, it wasn't long before we got tired of one another. But we never got as grouchy as the adults. It always seemed like everyone stayed until the last ounce of energy and excitement had faded. A stupor usually hung over the living room by 6 o'clock. When the ladies began covering up the Jell-O® salads it was like the work horn going off to release everyone from the labor of this curious ritual known as a holiday.

Unless something or someone changes, it will be the same next Thanksgiving. But for now, it's time to pack it up, head home and be thankful this happens only once a year.

ODE TO THE PARTY LINE

When I was 10 years old, my family and I lived in a small suburban neighborhood. The houses looked much the same: small ranch style homes with evenly cut lawns. By 1970's standards, we were neither rich nor poor.

However, you would think that we could have afforded our own telephone line. It must have saved my father all of $3 per month to be on the "Party Line" as opposed to a private line.

(For those who never had the privilege, a Party Line is just that: three or four other homes sharing the same line. You may pick up the phone and hear a dial tone at one point and a few moments later try to dial out again and instead of the dial tone, you would hear one of your

fellow partiers engrossed in their own conversation). I know, how inconvenient! Right? Well, for adults maybe, but for a young boy and his nine-year-old companion, this offered a standby activity when summer outdoor festivities got a little tiresome.

We pulled the same stunts (that's an adult word for an annoying child's antics) nearly every day. First, my buddy Mikey and I shared the receiver. We stood ear-to-ear so we could both hear and it wasn't long before heavy breathing or rude comments, for example, "is that so", began to pour out of our mouths. Immediately, we were greeted with the same daily response: "You kids cut that out. I've had just about enough." The more frustrated the tone, the more we liked it.

We also enjoyed the occasional clicking of the ringer. I actually learned this one from my mother who had waited over an hour one day just to call my Dad at work. I guess she figured that was long enough and sent her own message. If there's one thing kids enjoy, it's watching adults get crabby with one another.

Interestingly enough, Mikey and I were not limited just to our party line pals. We also knew what to do when we got a dial tone: get out the phonebook, pick a name that made us laugh and make "crank" calls. We only knew one: "Is your refrigerator running? You better go catch it!"

You would think after all the practice we had, our timing would be flawless, but Mikey got nervous every time it was his turn. He would either say the punch line too soon and too fast, or he would forget it altogether.

Can you image working around the house one afternoon when the phone rings and on the other side you hear a little boy's voice proclaim quickly, "Is your refrigerator running?" CLICK.

And no matter how badly Mikey performed, his response was always the same. He hopped around our kitchen on both feet excitingly all the while chanting, "How was that? How was that?" Hey, I was his buddy. What could I say? "Nice job!"

Caller ID has pretty much put a stop to this little number; however, there seems to be a new way of phone entertainment these days: "Smart" phones — phone antics for adults. People talk when they've nothing to say and say things that are left better unsaid ... and show photos that reflect an imaginary world that only exists online.

At least Mikey and I had an excuse; we were ornery little boys with nothing to do. But by the time we hit 10 or 11 years old, we grew out of it. Is your smart phone running? Maybe you should let it go.

THE LOOK AROUNDS

I grew up in a great place for a kid. Although at first glance it appeared to be just another '70s suburban neighborhood with matching houses lined up like a freight train, it was much more than that. It was alive with a heart and soul that pounded with passion from several boys and girls—big and small, athletic and non, creative and dull. We were all friends.

We enjoyed all of the four seasons with football and tag, hide-n-seek, snow forts and snowball fights. But summer brought life to a whole new level. Sure, we rode bikes, went swimming, played Little League baseball and the like; however, the greatest event of the season was camping out.

It happened on any given night all summer long. Frequently, the girls would stay over at Kim McQuen's house for a number of reasons: her parents were very cool and hardly interfered with any of our plans. In fact, I don't even remember what they looked like since I almost never saw them. Also, the McQuens had a wonderful screened-in porch that sat a good distance from the house—a great assist for many reasons ...

Kim's brothers, Jay and John, stayed at our place along with many of the other boys including Stevie Gonzalez, Mikey Burkholder and, of course, my brother Todd.

Our place was popular since our newly refurbished basement was not directly connected to our home. It had a wonderful garage entrance only—great for sneaking out at night without alarming the folks.

It's important to note that our midnight adventures were not born of a deviant agenda or mischief. "After midnight" offered a whole, wonderful world to us kids. Most of the time that world belonged to the elders, but with the moon up and the adults safely tucked in bed, the neighborhood belonged to us.

Around 1 or 2 in the morning, all of us boys would sneak out of our basement, out the back garage door and walk over to the McQuen's. We would whisper to

the girls through the screen, "Wake up - Wake up" as they would always be asleep when we arrived. Slowly, one by one, each would pass quietly through the door until all eight or nine of us departed for our late-night stroll.

Our entire gang would walk right down the middle of the street talking and laughing in a whisper. Occasionally, a real chuckle would bust out into the night followed by several quick shushes from the rest of us. Funny, as bold as we got, we never got caught. I suspected as we got older that a few of the parents knew, but they never let on.

Sometimes we would split up for a while. Mikey and I would share one of his Walkie-Talkies with Jay or my brother and we would chat from opposite sides of the neighborhood. We always used Mikey's Walkie-Talkies since his had a large, orange bar at the bottom for sending Morris Code. Now, none of us knew Morris Code, of course, but it was still a nice option to have.

We never grew tired of the nightly ritual; however, I do recall one night we went a bit too far. For some reason, Darlene, my neighborhood sweetheart, was not able to join us. I got the bright idea to go over and ring her doorbell at 2 in the morning. Although a few of the gang were hesitant—knowing if we got caught our nightly times of rendezvous were over—they reluctantly agreed.

Since I came up with the idea, you couldn't expect me to ring the bell too, could you? So we dared my brother Todd and John (the two oldest, about 11) to do it. As the rest of us hid behind a few trees at the edge of Darlene's property, Todd and John did their duty. In no time, they were back in our midst as we waited.

At first we questioned whether the bell was rung at all as nothing happened. Finally, Darlene's mother appeared at the door, fuzzy robe, hair in curlers and all. A few seconds later her husband, brave man that he was, showed up wearing his whitie-tighties and a confused look on his face.

They looked around the yard briefly, looked at each other and closed the door. Immediately, the girls headed for home and so did we—laughing all the way.

Funny, I never said anything to Darlene and she never said anything to me about it. I kind of expected her to. Maybe she didn't know. But that's as wild as we ever got and as funny as it was, we never rang a late-night bell again. But we did go to the McQuen's again, many times.

I can still feel the deliciously cool evening air and the excitement of walking with my friends down the

middle of the street under the midnight sky. What a wonderous time we shared—an adventure that was all ours and nobody else's.

Yes, in some ways, I still yearn for a delightful secret that can only be enjoyed with the innocence and imagination of a child-like heart.

TROY KIDDER

COACH'S KID

I grew up in a sports family. My Dad had been a college all-star in two sports and went on to teach and coach at an Indiana high school. From the time my brother, Todd who was two years my senior, and I were just little fellows we followed our father to countless practices and games for almost every sport as Dad was proficient in many.

As a result, that's all Todd and I knew. We seldom played with trucks or GI Joes or any of that stuff. We played sports. Fortunately, we lived in a suburban neighborhood with many boys and a few girls who were always ready for a game of baseball, football, basketball or even snowball fights in the Indiana winters. That too

takes athleticism. My brother and I both seemed to play most games with a "natural" ease.

And when we couldn't go outside for whatever reason, Todd and I took some white, athletic tape and mounted a large, old soup can to the basement wall and shot baskets with a tennis ball, or we threw tennis balls at each other.

Before you begin feeling really sad for my childhood experience, please keep in mind that it had its perks. Todd and I ran around the gym, football field and even baseball diamond like we owned them. Being the coach's kid had its advantages as the older boys treated us really well and always seemed to go out of their way to toss a ball or even a few jokes around with us. It was good.

Even in our neighborhood, I played with the older boys as most of our games included kids who were Todd's age or older. As a result, in those early years, I was all-time catcher or all-time hiker. I'll never forget the day my status changed in the neighborhood.

I'll never forget it for two reasons: first, it was Thanksgiving, and I was just eight years old. The relatives were at our house that year and per usual, by afternoon, the uncles were grumpy, and times were tough. That's when Todd and I got on the phone and found a few friends who needed some air as well.

Second, I remember it because for some reason instead of putting on my Converse "The Winner" tennis shoes, I pulled on an old pair of tan house slippers. I don't know why other than they felt comfortable and light and I felt faster. So before the Jell-O® salads were all gone, Todd and I were headed for the vacant lot—affectionately known as "The Field."

Normally, we could usually gather at least eight or ten players, but given the holiday, we felt thankful for the five or six we got. Per usual, I assumed my position as all-time hiker; however, destiny was on my side, or maybe it was the slippers on my feet, but my break came. Suddenly as Scott—one of the older boys who seldom even spoke to me—got desperate just before being tackled to the ground, he whipped me a pass. Although quite shocked at first, I caught the ball and started running like the dickens.

The pass surprised the others too as I quickly made it to the end zone for my first TD (Touch Down). My status had changed forever—I was a "gamer." As time progressed, I developed quite a reputation for having "great hands" and proved it on many occasions out there on "The Field."

Interestingly enough, despite Todd and my abilities to play several sports well, we both decided on basketball, and that's all we played by the time we hit high school. I do, however, recall an opportunity that presented itself for me to go back and relive some of those glorious gridiron days in the backyard—only this time on a grander scale.

It was fall, and I was a sophomore in high school. I had been hanging around the gym shooting some hoops and waiting for my Dad's football practice to finish because sometimes I joined a few of the guys for a harmless game of pitch and catch after practice. But this day was different as my father called me into the locker room while using his "Coaching Voice."

I followed quickly wondering what it could mean. When we got there, I noticed football equipment and a game jersey lying perfectly on the table. He said, "Son, your buddy Phil got hurt earlier today. He's okay, but he's out for a few games and maybe the rest of the season. We need a good wide receiver. We need you."

He paused to look at me for a moment to see how I responded. Then he continued, "You've always had great hands. You can do this. What do you say?"

I was stunned. I didn't want to disappoint him, but that idea/the opportunity couldn't break through my mindset of basketball only, and it couldn't break through my fears. I declined.

My Dad didn't mention it at home that night, and he never made the offer again. I missed the moment.

And hey, I'm well aware that it would not have led to a great pro or even college career. I was just a skinny kid who could catch a football. But I sure could have made a few memories and maybe even some magic with my teammates.

I bet you missed a few moments along the way as well. That's okay. We can learn from those days. We can set our resolve that we won't miss out on future opportunities to use some of those talents and abilities that lay dormant—sometimes for a lifetime.

So next time somebody offers that wild horse of opportunity, let's not settle in—let's saddle up!

TANE WAS HER NAME

I remember well moving into our farmhouse the summer I was ten years old. Funny, we had a barn, a chicken house and a little cornfield to the west of us. On the other side were a row of small houses leading to the tiny town of Millersburg.

It seems our new property sat directly on the "city" line. It was the best of both worlds as we enjoyed the beauty of the country and the blessing of neighbors as well.

The first neighbors I met were moving the very week we moved in. It seems their single mother had been renting a home two doors down from us and recently purchased a house in a nearby town.

Her kids, Tane and Darcy, were the first two I met since they were the first two I heard. As I carried moving boxes into the kitchen, a consistent car horn blared repeatedly in the distance. Naturally, I walked down the street to investigate.

A skinny girl with braces, Tane, sat in the front seat of the family's oldsmobuick stationwagon. She kept beeping the horn as her brother, Darcy, banged on the window pleading for her to stop. She didn't. So finally, he yelled, "Honk your brains out. I'm going in."

Later that evening I met the two and heard from other friends that the afternoon episode was standard procedure for these two. Tane was two years my senior and Darcy just a year. We chatted briefly, and I liked them. A few days later they were gone.

This was tough to take. I had just moved in and already some kids I liked moved out. Besides, there were only four or five other kids on my side of the overpass (into town) and I felt even more lonely.

However, that was not the last of the dynamic duo. They would return summers—sometimes for a few days and sometimes for a few weeks as they stayed with their grandparents who lived across the street from us.

I looked forward to those times. And so did the others on our side of the tracks. Our little neighborhood came alive when they arrived.

During the day it was all sorts of things like wiffleball and dodgeball. We acted out made up plays and sang songs. We even ate our bologna sandwiches together under the large shade tree in our front yard. Darcy and Terry (our other neighbor who was never any fun at all unless Darcy and Tane were around) climbed the trees as high as they could go until we got scared and begged them to come down. Darcy and Terry were always trying to come up with something new for us to do.

And at night it was kick the can and scary stories under the stars. And sometimes after it got really late, we would retreat to one of our homes for board games and popcorn. It was grand.

By the time I turned 14 and Tane 16, we looked around and none of the other gang could be found. Darcy seldomly came anymore. The others I guess had grown up or had just grown out of it. So there we were. Even though on occasion we could stir up a rousing game of kick the can, it wasn't the same. But for me, it was still good.

Sure, I had a crush on Tane—I had since that first day. And if she knew, she never let on, and she never treated me like a little brother either. Besides, I was aware of my place in the universe. I knew that attractive 16-year-old girls don't have romantic inclinations toward 14-year-old boys especially this one who wore the same shorts and tank top every day (Oh, wait. I still do that in the summer). It was more important than that anyway; we were friends.

When you spend that much time together though some people will draw their own conclusions. I recall one time that Tane and I road our bikes across the overpass into town for a little lunch. We stopped off at the Handy Pantry—a local hang out that was half grocery store and half restaurant.

As we walked in, Steve quickly greeted me (an older boy, not necessarily my friend) with wide eyes and a smile. He asked, "Is that your girlfriend?" I didn't want to lie but I also appreciated the newfound respect, so I said nothing and walked on … Hey, a junior high boy has got to find self esteem boosters where they can be found.

Well, that's about all the mileage I got out of that one especially since by summer's end it would be quite a while before Tane or Darcy would visit our tiny little town.

In fact, I remember the last time we would be together before going our separate ways—for whatever reason. Darcy called me one autumn evening and asked if he and Tane could pick me up for a movie and pizza. Shocked, I said sure. By now I was 16 and in the middle of my high school experience as Tane and Darcy were closing in on the end of theirs.

We had a great night together. I don't recall the movie or the food, but the ride home was like old times. Darcy and I both squeezed into the front seat with Tane as she drove and together we sang along with a Donna Summer 8-track (Hey, it was still the disco era). Darcy was as crazy as ever whipping his head around and singing at the top of his lungs like a girl.

He would also reach over at times and grab the steering wheel, and this time it was him honking the horn which prompted Tane to do a little crazy-girl screaming of her own, "Stop, you big jerk!" Yes, it was good to see that some things never change.

And in my memory those fantastic friends live on, but as they were then—young, imaginative, innocent and free. No, I don't think of those days often, but when I do, I thank God for Tane, Darcy and the others, and hope that somehow, deep down, they know how much they meant to me.

TROY KIDDER

'YES, MRS. BARTHOLAMEW'

I remember the summer between my sophomore and junior years of high school. I worked detasseling corn as I had done since I was 13 years old (For those who did not grow up in the Midwest, detasseling was the process of removing the tassel of a corn stock to keep it from pollinating the rest of the seed corn).

In the morning the corn was often wet and cold. If you wore jeans, they were wet and soggy in the morning and they would stick to you by afternoon and begin to itch. For the rookies in the bunch, some would get cuts on their arms and legs as the corn leaves could slash skin like a razor. And others would get corn rash (not unlike poison ivy) and have to quit.

I remember that my mother bought me a long, rain poncho to protect me from the hazards of morning corn. At first, being a teenager, I refused to wear it, but as time went on, I used it in the morning and wore shorts in the afternoon. It was sure better than those jeans.

Despite the uncomfortable inconveniences, I learned to enjoy working in the fields. Usually, each "crew" consisted of six members and a crew chief. Since I had put in three summers previously, I got promoted to crew chief that summer. It was alright. The money was okay too as I got a bump in pay with my new position. I now earned 50 cents an hour above the minimum wage ($3.35 in the early '80s).

Prior to all this advancement, I needed money that summer as detasseling didn't start until mid-summer. That made Principal Bose's call even more of a blessing.

Shortly after school ended for the summer, the principal, a golf buddy of my father, received a call from a gentlemen seeking someone to handle lawn care duties for his aging mother. He recommended me. It turns out that she lived just a few miles from us and on the same country road.

I agreed to meet with her and see if it was a fit. It paid only $7 but gas and mower were supplied—and besides, the yard was very small considering that it was an old farmhouse with a barn. The woman seemed nice too. However, she was very old and had a patch over her left eye from a recent surgery.

I'll never forget the first time I mowed that yard. I was rolling along on this ancient lawn mower—at least it was a rider—lost in thought, and I failed to see Mrs. Bartholamew running along behind me trying desperately to get my attention.

She had been calling out "Troy, Troy." I turned off the mower and after she caught her breath, she continued, "Troy, don't forget the backyard. It needs done, too."

I said, "Yes, Mrs. Bartholamew, I know. I just got started. Don't worry. I will do it all." I continued on my merry way and as I finished the front and headed toward the small side yard by the barn, I got that funny feeling again that someone was following me. Yep. It was her …

"… Troy, don't forget the backyard." Again, I said, "Don't worry. I will do it all. Please just relax."

Well, this went on four or five times before I finally finished. Upon completion, I went to the door and she promptly paid me the $7. She offered me a glass of cold water and some not-so-homemade cookies—which I accepted. And sometimes we even talked for a while.

Assuming that since this was the first time and she would eventually trust me, I believed the pattern would end. As you may have guessed, it didn't. It was the same every time I mowed the yard that summer.

In fact, a couple of times, I tired of the game and pretended not to see her. But guilt won out because although she slowed down, she never quit. I could see her out of the corner of my eye. Of course, she was only running by definition as she kept her arms high and rotating like a sprinter—huffing and puffing. And that patch over her eye was flapping in the wind. But her feet barely moved enough to be considered a walk. I stopped.

To be sure, Mrs. Bartholamew was a quirky, older lady, but she wasn't crazy. Apparently at some point, her yard had not gotten done the way she wanted it and that fear never left her.

Funny, over the past few years, when my wife reminds me of the obvious, I always say, "Yes, Mrs. Bartholamew." And when I point out that which needs no explanation, she says the same to me.

This may sound like a joke at the expense of one of our elders. And maybe it is a bit; however, the older I get the more I realize the perceptions of the things that happened to me—and even those around me—are difficult to divide out what's real and what just feels real because they are stuck in my craw.

I think most of us from time to time run around our own yard repeating ourselves trying to bring comfort and control to a situation that feels dangerously close to a place in our soul that was violated or maybe something just went terribly wrong.

Like Mrs. Bartholamew, that doesn't make us crazy, just human.

THE COLLEGE YEARS

THE LOSS OF SOMEONE I NEVER KNEW

As autumn changes our world to cool evenings and colorful mornings—reds and yellows delicately dancing to the ground in a patterned swirl—occasional warm breezes send me softly to summers gone by.

Sometimes I slip back to the summer before my sophomore year in college. I was working for the street department in Millersburg. I guess I was the street department. A town of about 800, Millersburg had only my boss Robin who was police chief, fire chief, head of the sewer department and anything else that needed doing. I was his assistant.

It was a great job! Robin taught me to work a pay loader, a dump truck and a backhoe. After spilling

several loads of dirt on the ground en route to the dump truck and after almost running over a small shed (which shouldn't have been there in the first place, I might add) with the pay loader, I have to count Robin as one of the most patient men I've ever known.

On Fridays, it was my job to broom-sweep the entire Main Street. Except for an occasional surprise left by the horse power of our Amish neighbors, the task was not unpleasant. The elders would often visit with me, offering tales of this tiny town. Or as we looked up at the rays of the summer sun splashing through the maple trees, we just stood there quietly, sharing a summertime moment in the shade. It was here that I began to feel a part of this town, a place where I was known and where I belonged.

I remember one August afternoon in particular. I was at the park painting the last of the fire hydrants fluorescent orange. Summer was coming to an end, and I was finishing my last project before heading back to college.

I had just returned from lunch. Covering myself in sun-tan oil, I pulled on my radio headset and quickly became engrossed in my work . . . I was feeling good. Suddenly an ear-piercing scream burst through the gentle beat of my "mellow classics" radio station. At first

I was upset that anyone would disturb my contentment. Then I realized that a lady was running toward me yelling, "Get the police! He's dead! He's dead!" After seeing where the woman was frantically gesturing, I jumped up and ran as hard as I could toward downtown. At that moment, Robin turned toward me in the police car. He picked me up and I pointed the way.

As we pulled into the driveway, I could see a car backed up to the house. A hose was attached to the tailpipe and run into the house. We broke through the front door, and Robin said, "You'd better stay here." He soon came back from the bedroom and said, "He's dead. It's suicide." I stood there for a second, then slowly walked out into the sunshine. The sledgehammer of death had pounded its way into a soft summer day.

Robin took me to the clerk's office and told me I could go home when I wanted. I sat there in silence, pondering the loss of someone I'd never known. Summer had ended for me that day. Somehow things would never be the same for me again—and maybe, too, for this little Indiana town.

ONE-SWAN POND

It was the summer of '85 and I was preparing for my senior year in college. Fortunately, I landed a good job as groundskeeper for a family just outside of Goshen, Indiana.

They owned a large house on a hill that overlooked a small meadowland—and a pond with one swan in it. I called it "One-Swan Pond." In addition to the meadow, there were extensive grounds to mow, including winding trails through 600 acres of wildlife preserve. This was my favorite portion to mow.

Often I would set out early in the morning to mow the trails; seldom disappointing me were the deer at dawn. Grouped in what appeared to be little families, they would stand on, or along, the trail. As the sputtering tractor edged ever closer, they leaped into the woods, not to be seen again the rest of the day.

The serene tableau is still imprinted on my mind's eye: ground glistening as the rising sun shot rays across the morning dew; birds of every kind and color singing; ground hogs, chipmunks and mice dashing and playing— all of God's creation applauding the new day.

I would breathe in deeply and know I was blessed as I headed back to the house for some other chores. I was learning new jobs daily. My newest was to feed the swan of One-Swan Pond. It sounded simple: Just get the swan food out of the garage (where in the world do you buy food for a swan?) and put it in the swan feeder by the pond.

As I began filling the feeder, I noticed the swan swimming my direction. I didn't pay much attention to it as I picked up the bag of food and began to walk back up the hill. Suddenly, I heard a sound and as I looked back, that bird was coming toward me—full speed. I took off running and slipped and fell, spilling the feed. I looked again, and that naughty fowl tried to "whap" me with its wings. I got away but left the feed on the ground. As I stood atop the hill, my heart pounding, I stared at

this beautiful, sculpted creature swimming effortlessly in the pond, wondering what had just happened.

Later that day, we crossed paths again when I had to mow the grass surrounding the pond. At first, I didn't pay much attention, but then it became obvious that the swan was swimming parallel with me and the John Deere mower. All the while, since swans have eyes on each side of their head, it was watching me.

When I'd head the other direction, it would turn automatically, like an electronic duck in a shooting gallery. Maybe I saw it in those terms because I was mad—mad because I realized it was trying to intimidate me, and it was doing a pretty good job.

As I rolled along on the John Deere, I began to think (there's plenty of time to reflect when you sit on a mower all day) that we're not much different from that swan. We put up walls. Sometimes we flap our little arms and give the "evil eye" to protect our "space." After all, it's easier to exert control than it is to trust others and have faith.

Well, that's the lesson I learned at One-Swan Pond—and I guess I'm still learning it.

TROY KIDDER

MOTOR TO THE MEADOW

The balmy breezes of spring carry the sweet smell of wet grass freshly cut, sunny days with nothing but short sleeves and shorts, and cool nights quietly filled with starry wonders.

During college years when I would return home in early spring, I would religiously watch the sunset from atop our small chicken house, or I'd hop on my Kawasaki 125 and head to a quiet place I had discovered years before.

It was a few miles from our home down a seldom-traveled country road. It was on the left just before reaching some old railroad tracks where weeds grew between the rails. There lay a glorious clover field that gave way to a western woods. I would sit on my cycle and watch as the sun sank slowly toward the timber

and settled in behind the trees. Some of the golden rays, now orange with age, pushed past the trees to play in the pasture one more time before fading to amber glow.

I would stay until night had chased the last lingering light from the sky, and then I would ride home reflectively in the darkness.

I remember the last time I raced down that road on my motorbike. It was late spring, and I had just finished my junior year in college. I couldn't wait to get on my bike and head for my meadow. By the time I unpacked, the sun had begun to set. I ran to the barn for my bike and, since the day had been warm, it was just me in a T-shirt, a pair of cut-off sweat pants—and my bare feet tucked into an old pair of Chuck Taylor high-tops.

My bike started on first kick as always, and I rolled out of our driveway. The warm spring air whispered past my face with just a hint of the night to come. I breathed in with joy on approaching the familiar road leading to my place of peace.

But as I slowed to turn, the motor fluttered, for the cycle had sat unridden all winter. So I decided to "wind it out" to clear the winter clutter. I leaned forward as my speed climbed from 40 to 50 and now 60. The bike was not built for speed, and it began to shake as I exceeded 70 mph.

My hands clenched tightly to the handlebars, my eyes squinted and my hair blew straight behind my head. This basically defenseless boy was pushing ever faster down the paved but bumpy country road.

Suddenly, at 77 mph, I heard a click in the transmission—and just as quickly recalled a friend's words of wisdom, "If you ever hear a click in your gears, pull in the clutch." It rang in my head like an order, and I responded instantly.

At that same moment the transmission blew out and, with clutch and brake in, I screeched erratically to a halt. Pulse racing, I sat there in the dim evening light, my mind chasing out images of "what if."

It was a long walk that night as my motorcycle resisted every push on that three-mile journey home. The night air rubbed coldly on my bare skin, but I didn't care. I was alive.

I pondered many things on the way home, but one thing I was sure of: Though we as human beings may make mistakes, we are no accident. We are here for a purpose, and every life is a gift. Such a gift must not be taken for granted. These truths hit home for me one spring evening of my youth.

RISE 'N' SHINE, DAVE

Each spring as the local high school seniors graduate, I think of how many in turn will prepare for the challenges of college—a learning experience both in and out of the classroom. For example, sharing a matchbox-sized room with someone very different from yourself.

Dave was my roommate my sophomore through senior years of college. Dave came from South Bend, and I was from a small rural area—the "barnyard," as Dave put it. Our differences went far beyond our old neighborhoods. In fact, the biggest one landed right there in our dorm room. I liked the room clean and organized, and he had no concept of either. Instead of keeping his clothes in the dressers that were nicely provided for us, he kept a pile of clothes in front of his closet, which was situated directly behind our entry door.

Some days returning from class, I would have to push with force (shoulder firmly planted on door and "plow") to get me and my book bag through the doorway—since his pile had grown. Another reason "the pile" was so upsetting was that he really didn't use it. As repulsive as it may sound, every morning Dave would take the same brown corduroys and blue-and-red flannel shirt from atop the pile. Then he would pull on his yellow "Millersburg Farmers' Day" hat I had given him, and he would head to class. It was the same every morning except Sundays when, of course, he didn't wear the hat.

The interesting thing is that when Dave would go home every now and then he'd load the entire pile into large, green army sacks and take it home to be washed. When he returned Sunday night, he unloaded the clean pile directly onto the same spot on the floor.

Finally, as you can imagine, we had quite a discussion about "the pile." One which included plenty of yelling, name calling and some object throwing (I did not want to get hit by anything from that pile). When the proverbial dust had settled, we reached a compromise. It didn't end the life of "the pile," but Dave did agree to relocate it to the closet. From that point on, he would pull it out every morning, grab the usual garb and shove the whole thing back into the closet. He became quite efficient at this.

Another of our differences had to do with his utter distaste for mornings. I was a morning person, and Dave was not. I liked to talk in the morning, and Dave did not. In fact, he was anything but subtle about quieting me down in the mornings. For example, any talking brought grunts of disapproval; whistling elicited sharp "shut ups"; and sometimes my happy humming brought borderline profanity.

I wasn't the only sound in the morning Dave didn't like. The other was his alarm clock and mine. Dave would usually set his clock for 7:30 when he had an 8 o'clock class; however, he never got up at this time. It became a morning ritual: His alarm would go off and within a split second, no matter what position he was in, he would smack that snooze button and go right back to sleep. This went on three or four times every morning before he finally got up. It was quite annoying when I wanted to sleep in, but it was an amazing thing to behold to see someone in a deep sleep hit the snooze button so instantaneously with such accuracy.

I remember one morning in particular. I decided to get up extremely early to work on a paper. I awoke before my alarm went off and headed for the showers. When I returned, I tiptoed in and saw Dave sleeping soundly. As I quietly dressed, I glanced up toward my alarm to check the time; the clock wasn't there. I looked around the room before noticing it lying in pieces near the wall on the floor. Almost a college graduate at this point, I used my deductive-reasoning skills and concluded that the alarm had gone off while I was in the shower. Dave had turned it off for me.

Sometimes, whether we are bunk-to-bunk in a dorm room, or door-to-door in a community, it's good to clear the air. But after our emotions are laid bare, it's time to move toward common ground. Then maybe we'll discover, just as Dave and I did, that with a little effort we'll find much more to agree on than disagree. Dave is one of my best friends to this day.

'YOU WOULDN'T DARE'

It was my junior year at Taylor University when I witnessed a scene of what might be termed unwarranted daring. I remember the situation well. It started when my roommate and I left our third-floor dorm room and headed toward the Dining Commons for lunch. It was May, and the last week of finals had begun.

This trip was slightly different from our usual noontime ritual, as Dave was carrying our one-gallon pitcher in hopes of obtaining a free fill-up of milk. If there's one thing a college student needs during finals, in addition to pizza, it's plenty of milk and coffee. The beverages simply had to be there to wash down the enormous quantities of Oreos and Chips Ahoy cookies being consumed all night long—a college student's soul food, especially when the studying was constant.

After a quick lunch, Dave and I enjoyed a "one time only" complimentary gallon of milk. The cooks told us this with a smile because we had been the only ones to approach them. However, it came with a warning, "Don't ask again."

Heading for our room, we were feeling free, the sun reminding us that summer was but a week away. We quickly wove through the traffic of would-be lunchers and, having filled the pitcher to the brim, the other students happily made room. There were smiles and yells of delight: "Whoa!" "What do you guys got there?" and "Hey, wait a second, I'll get my cup." Others simply laughed and commented to friends.

Soon we were heading up the stairs toward our room, moving quickly but carefully, not wanting to spill a precious drop. As we opened the door to the third floor, Doug Samson was on his way out, and we almost collided. We all started to laugh as we realized the potential of what almost happened.

And it would have been especially costly for Doug, a friend, but not a close one. He always wore the trendiest outfits, and this day was no different for "Dapper Doug." Golf shirt, stylish Bermuda shorts, white tennis shoes.

Well, after a quick chuckle, we were all about to head on our way when Dave, standing directly in front of Doug, tilted the pitcher toward him jokingly as if he were going to dump it on him. Doug's laughter and jovial smile transformed to a stiff upper lip and protruded chest. This caught Dave and me off guard. Then Doug went a step further and sternly warned, "You wouldn't dare!"

Dave rotated slightly toward his right, still with a puzzled look on his face, but he seemed to be asking me for final approval to do what we both now knew must happen. I just covered my face with my hand. This motion seemed to be the trigger. Dave rotated back toward Doug and, in one single motion of force, heaved the entire gallon of milk on him.

It splashed with fury against Doug's chest and chin. And as the cold liquid hit him, he didn't even move. He stood there quietly for a second, looking himself over. Then in disbelief he began to repeat, "He did it. I can't believe he did it."

Slowly, Doug turned toward the hallway and began to walk—with stiff legs now that the milk was making its way into his pin-striped Bermudas. As he disappeared down the hall, his refrain continued: "I can't believe he did it."

As Dave and I sat in our dorm room pondering the loss of our beloved liquid, we both agreed that Doug needed the milk more than we did, and we were all too willing to make the sacrifice.

Doug made a choice to rise up in pride, and he paid the price. I think of the times I myself have paraded in pride, and someone had to "rain" on me. It may not have been milk, but it still wasn't a pretty sight. But I think we all need that from time to time in order to remind us that everyone is just human. We're all frail. And no one is better than anyone else.

You've heard it said that pride comes before a fall. It's true! But we have an opportunity to change and not have to face the fall. All we have to do is humble ourselves, or a pitcher of milk just may be the "refresher" to keep us on course.

EVERYONE NEEDS AN AMY

I really got to know Amy the summer I took Driver's Education at the high school we were attending. She, Jay, Sandy and I shared a Ford Granada, along with our instructor, Mr. Weaver.

Amy was a blond-haired, blue-eyed farm girl. The fact that she had spent at least some time on her daddy's tractors made it somewhat perplexing that she was scared out of her mind to drive—not to mention the rest of us when she was behind the wheel.

I'll never forget the time Mr. Weaver had us out exploring the forgotten farms of Amish country (he felt safer way out there, I guess), and Amy was driving. We were cruising a country road as straight as an Amishman's row of beans when we happened upon a slow-moving duck truck (a truck loaded with ducks).

Mr. Weaver nonchalantly told Amy to pass. She started swerving to the right out of fear, and I heard the thump, thump of weeds whapping my side of the Granada. Finally, Mr. Weaver got her calm enough to pull into the passing lane. She didn't speed up, just pulled into the other lane. With a little more encouragement, she began to accelerate and actually pass the duck truck.

With mission accomplished, she eased into the proper lane only to fade too far right, and again it began: the chorus of weeds—thump, thump, thump against the Granada. This flustered Amy, and she let her foot completely off the accelerator. I looked out the back window only to see M-A-C-K closing in quickly. HONK! HONK! There's nothing like a semi's air horn to strike fear into the hearts of those just ahead.

Jay and I both screamed, "Speed up!" Mr. Weaver grabbed her knee, pushing her foot firmly into the accelerator. The Granada sputtered, then speeded us away from danger. We simultaneously drew a sigh of relief. And all of us said, "Oh, Amy."

That wasn't all for Amy and me. And even though being around Amy offered some risk to life and limb, we became "buds." She was the self-proclaimed "airhead,"

and school was always more fun when she was around. Graduation day found us good friends if not best.

As we went off to separate colleges, we stayed in touch, writing letters filled with laughter, poems, stories of exams and loves lost. And on occasion, we'd meet, and Amy would have me off to some faraway coffeehouse where long-haired men played old Beatles tunes, and we debated politics and religion deep into the night.

Sure, Amy was the original cutup, but she had the verbal firepower to blast opinions and mindsets right out of the water. I enjoyed that very much. But best of all, Amy was quirky.

I'll never forget one late summer evening . . . Amy called me about 11 o'clock. She asked if I had heard of the new overpass opening in our town. She went on to say that didn't such an occasion call for a celebration? I made the mistake of agreeing and, by midnight, Amy and I were atop the new overpass in Goshen, Indiana . . .

With guitar in hand, I played, and we sang old John Denver tunes ("Rocky Mountain High" and "Take Me Home, Country Roads") from the illustrious sidewalk that runs alongside the overpass. To top it off, Amy refused to leave until a train passed below. Fortunately, one did before any valiant men in blue took us downtown for questioning.

Amy thought outside the box. Shoot, she lived outside the box and, although we didn't always agree (many times not), she allowed me to express myself in quirky ways too without criticism or condemnation. That's honor. And when I came to her and said I wanted to propose marriage to a young lady I had known but seven weeks, she encouraged me to follow my heart, while others hassled me, trying to get me to give up the idea altogether. (Lori and I have been happily married for many years.) No, the honor of a friend like Amy is not just the memories—no matter how grand— it's the labor, the gifts and the contributions to whom we are now and, even more importantly, to whom we will become.

HAPPY BIRTHDAY TO ME

It was January '86, second semester of my senior year at Taylor University.

I remember standing in the Dining Commons, tray in hand, looking for a familiar face when a threesome saw me and invited me to join their table. I accepted and was introduced to Sherri and her friends, John and Kim. Soon it was discovered that Sherri and I were from the same area (me, from Millersburg). The other two were out-of-staters.

Before long we were laughing, sharing Christmas break stories and just plain having a good time. I even remember complaining that since my birthday is a week before Christmas, I never got much except the traditional 3-pack of white, all–cotton briefs complete with racing stripes across the top of the elastic band. In a moment of whimsy, I announced that my birthday was now May 18 instead. With no major holidays nearby, I joked that from then on I fully expected a dramatic change in my relatives' gift giving.

Although we parted friends that day, months went by with only an occasional "hello" here and there across campus. Spring had sprung quickly and found me one week from graduation, not necessarily tiptoeing through the tulips. I had recently ended a long-term relationship with my high school sweetheart (leaving some of my friends and relatives baffled) and then shared some unwanted relationship advice with my roommate of three years who responded with the silent treatment. Or was it the fact that I had stepped on his head during a game of one-on-one basketball?

Anyhow, the pressure we seniors were feeling, I think, was that of leaving this sheltered world of semi-reality and realizing it was time to grow up and get a "real job." It was at this time that I heard from my once lunchtime friends. When Sherri called me that Saturday afternoon I was knee-deep in a six-page paper. She asked if I could spare some room in my pickup truck when we headed home the following week. I said sure, and then she casually invited me to join her and the "gang" (John

and Kim) for church and lunch. I declined due to a deadline on my paper, but Sherri's persistence resulted in a compromise plan of them picking me up for lunch.

I was up a good part of the night working on my paper and managed to finish just before the doorbell rang. I greeted two grinning girls in gowns and a smirking Johnny in his Sunday best. There I stood in grey sweat pants, a plain T-shirt and my yellow Millersburg Farmers' Day hat covering my curly mop. I asked for a few minutes to clean up. They said "no time" and I was quickly ushered into the car.

As we entered the Dining Commons, I got some stares from those dressed in their best and was paraded past everyone to a corner table decorated with party favors and colorfully wrapped gifts. In complete bewilderment I said, "What in the world is this?" They laughed and echoed, "Don't you know what day this is?...May 18! Happy Birthday!"

I sat down, quietly astonished. As I gazed, somewhat dazed for a moment, they began pushing gifts towards me with glee. I got fun little things, including a full-pound bag of peanut M&M®'s (a college student's soul food). Not a 3-pack of white, all-cotton briefs in sight.

As I looked into the dancing, delighted eyes of these special friends, trying to figure what I could have possibly done to deserve such a gift, I realized what it truly is to be "more blessed to give than receive." And I realized that as difficult as it was at first for me to accept, this was my time to receive, and what a blessing it was.

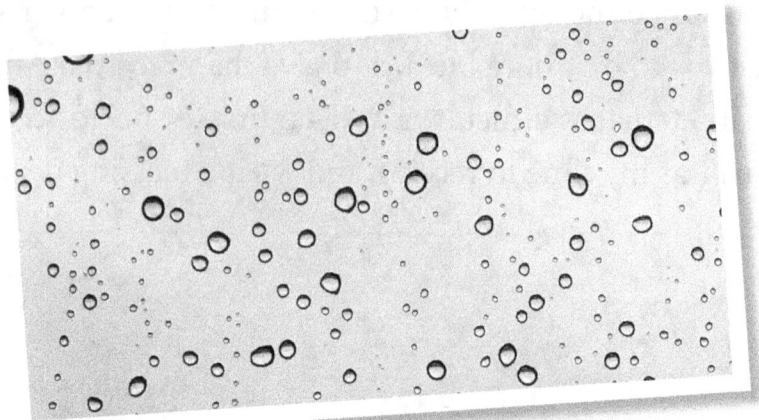

SOMETHING MORE FRAGILE THAN GLASS

The summer between my junior and senior years in college I was working as a groundskeeper for a millionaire and his family. They owned a large home, with extensive grounds, nestled cozily in the country.

It was a great place to work. Days were filled with odd jobs and hours atop a large lawn tractor, my sun-soaked skin turning brown. Often as I putt-putted along, I pondered my future. I would begin student teaching in the fall and, by spring, I'd be a college graduate ready to take on the world—well, at least the educational world.

I looked good. I felt good. Everything seemed to be fine.

I recall one afternoon in particular. I returned home (my parents' home) from an enjoyable day's work. I kicked off my grungy duds and hopped into the shower. There in the familiar farmhouse of my youth, I showered off the dust and residue from a day in the summer sun. I shut off the shower feeling refreshed.

I pushed to open the shower door, but it wouldn't budge. This didn't faze me, since it had happened in the past on several occasions. I quickly reverted to Plan B, which was to rotate my hips and smack my rear end against the glass shower door to pop it open.

When this failed to work, without hesitation, I rotated again more swiftly. As my skinny little backside hit the door, the glass door exploded onto the bathroom floor, onto me, and all over the shower.

I stood there helplessly as I watched various parts of my body begin to bleed: my feet, my right thigh, and a few other places here and there. But that wasn't the worst of it… What do I do now?

I couldn't step down because there was glass everywhere, and it would certainly cause more bleeding. I knew that my Mother was in the kitchen, but I was way beyond the age of calling out for "Mommy," especially with nothing more than a towel around my

waist. I reflected some more as the blood began to drip off my toes and onto the shattered glass.

Finally, a thought! "Daaaaddd? Oh, Dad!" I felt I was calling out calmly, but it was with enough intensity to cause my Mother to find my Father quickly. Soon Dad arrived. At first, he only peeked in. I'll never forget the look on his face. He looked at me. He looked at the floor. He looked at the broken door. With nothing more than a blank expression and a monotone voice, he said, "Don't move son. I'll get this picked up first."

So I stood there in all awkwardness and some embarrassment as my father cleared the way for my exit from the shower. As it turned out, my injuries were minor, and no scars would form, since no stitches were needed. However, something bothered me for some time after that…

There in the midst of my youth, strength and hope, I got a glimpse of reality. I got a glimpse of my human frailty.

THE ADULT YEARS

LUNCH WITH THE S&B CLUB

Having started my teaching career right out of college at age 22, I managed to do some things over the years that raised a few eyebrows—especially among the "more mature" educational instructors. Please keep in mind that most of my "antics" were not born of rebellion or evil agenda. Most of them can be attributed to sheer youthful exuberance, even goofiness, not to mention a certain reluctance to mindlessly follow the status quo.

I managed, however, to burn a few bridges along the way during my 10-year teaching career. It wasn't limited to one or two incidents; one might say there was a bit of a pattern. In my early years of teaching, for example, my wardrobe seemed to be the topic of much conversation (behind closed doors, of course, and not mine). I often

sported jeans with a fine suit coat purchased at the local Goodwill store for $3. (This may have been less for style points and more due to my $16,500 annual salary.)

I learned through the grapevine (and most schools have great grapevines) that my classroom activities also rocked a few boats, as stories apparently circulated among students and teachers alike. I liked to bring in props to class (some also purchased at Goodwill). I wore a construction hardhat on sentence-building days; yelled the eight parts of speech through a bull horn; and carried an old World War II leather attaché case ($1-guess where?). I scarcely have space to mention the songs I sang while standing atop my desk, my toast tossing and my telling of countless stories, including my personal favorite, "The (Harley) Hogs of Amish Country."

Despite some creative teaching moments, looking back, I really don't consider myself an outstanding educator. It was too hard for me to keep an edge every day. I was, however, pretty good at marketing. As yearbook adviser, this skill came in handy. Not only did it provide opportunities for me outside the teaching profession, it eventually became the proverbial straw that broke the camel's back in regard to some of my colleagues.

Due to creative marketing campaigns year after year, more than once my student staff and I ended up on the local television news and a number of radio stations as well. As our profits soared into the thousands of dollars, some folks—the "elders" of our fine school—had heard enough. They were better known as the self-proclaimed "S&B Club." The "S" stands for stitch and the "B" rhymes with it. (Yep, you got it!)

This group (made up mostly of women teachers with more than 15 years of experience) met for lunch nearly every day in the Home Economics room just down the hall from the cafeteria. They would bring in cookies and chips to add to the school lunches on a tray.

Having a dear friend who was a card-carrying member, I had known for years that my name was being raked over the coals (along with a few others', of course). So during the spring of my last year teaching, it occurred to me that it would only be proper for me to stop in and "do lunch" with some of my fellow staff members.

I'll never forget the day I carried my lunch tray into the Home Economics room (a little late for making a dramatic entrance). It seemed to be a happy day, as I heard much chatter coming from the little Home Ec

room. But as I walked in, all conversations stopped, and a couple of jaws hit the floor.

I greeted everyone with a cheery "Hello," asked if I could join them (I saw at least one nod) and sat down. Slowly, conversation picked up again, and (to my delight) I heard no negative talk about anyone. Just to prove it wasn't a one-time fluke, I made a few more visits before the year was over.

Looking back, I have to laugh at my boldness and at the teachers' reactions. But this is not a critique on the behavior of teachers. This happens every day in businesses and factories alike. People love to talk. People love to criticize. And yes, people love to gossip.

But what if I had handled things differently? What if I had made that trip to the Home Ec room years earlier— not to save face, defend myself or even hinder them from talking about me? What if I had come in just to let them know that we were all on the same team and that they could count on me?

Then, instead of just a story that brings a few others and me a chuckle, I would be a living example of someone who dared show a little humility and strength of character.

THE BIKE OF MY YOUTH

When I was 16 years old, I wanted a car, but I didn't have enough cash, so I settled for a Kawasaki 125 motorbike. I purchased it from an Amish man for just $220. He seemed in a hurry to part with it, and I asked no questions.

Shortly thereafter, I went exploring. I discovered the beauty of creation as I wandered the old country roads winding through Amish country. I rode dirt-bike trails on the farms of friends and watched the setting sun from the edge of a clover field that rolled to a western woods.

I came alive those next few summers that I owned that motorbike. And just recently as I drove by the local Kawasaki dealership, those feelings came rushing back . . . Right there in front of the dealership, between a

four-wheeler and a monstrous road machine, stood a Kawasaki K-100 reminiscent of the motorbike of my youth. I pulled in, looked it over and sat on it. I must have grown since my early 20s because this thing seemed small, but I didn't care. I had to have it.

It took two weeks of my heart arguing with my head until finally one morning not long ago I decided to buy that machine. By 3 o'clock that afternoon I had me a motorbike very similar to the bike of my teens. This time, however, instead of living on a farm on the outskirts of Amish country, I now lived in the suburbs just outside of town.

What will the neighbors think? Oh, who cares! I wanted to ride. The first couple of days were pretty smooth. I was having a great time. The wind was warm and the ride a little reckless, but I got better. None of my neighbors were around to see, or so I thought. One afternoon as I rode down our street a neighbor came running out of his house toward me, his arms waving wildly as if to flag me down. My first thought was that he must be in some kind of trouble. But as I slowed down and he drew near, a big smile broke across his face. Mike, who may be in his late 30s or early 40s, began to chatter like we were old pals or something. I had spoken to him briefly once in the past six months. Amazingly enough, he began to tell me how he had been thinking about getting a little bike of his own to tool around on.

He went on to say that he had never owned one, but his childhood neighbors did—and he had ridden theirs. He had seen me ride around the 'hood, and he got inspired.

So much for shame. I was a retro hero inspiring childlike joy in at least one of my neighborhood "buddies." Interestingly enough, another of my neighbors had just bought a bike as well; however, his is a Harley Davidson Softtail Standard 1450. (I don't exactly know what that means, but it's downright scary-looking.)

Don is his name, and the bike fits him well. He's a former high school football star with a protruding chest and sculpted military 'do. Sometimes he works outside with his shirt off. If my wife and I happen to drive by during that time, I quickly get her attention and point the other direction. (You can't have your wife thinking that men are supposed to look like that.)

Don's a nice guy, and we talk on occasion. One day while he was working in his yard (shirt on), I pulled into his driveway with my little Kawasaki. He came over quickly and began to give my bike a good once-over.

He said, "Wow, I like it. I thought I saw a dirt bike in your garage the other day." (I decided that, since he liked my bike, I wouldn't make a fuss about him peeking into my garage.)

Feelin' good, I suggested that he and I go riding sometime. I was kind of joking, but Don joined right in with "Hey, let's do it."

I said, "But it's kind of small."

He said, "A bike's a bike, and I'll ride with you."

"Cool."

Well, we haven't gone yet, but we will. And although we may not start a Saturday afternoon motorcycle club—besides, the "Meadowridge Riders" or "Old Orchard Bikers" doesn't sound real cool or tough—I've learned a lot. If I don't take myself too seriously, others aren't quite as uptight and judgmental as I thought.

All in all, life is grand, and the neighbors are okay too.

So get on your bike and ride.

TROY KIDDER

LIVIN' FROM ONE COUNTRY SONG TO ANOTHER

I remember one chilly spring weeknight recently. I had run out of milk for my late-night bowl of cereal (preferably whole milk on Fruity Pebbles) and decided to head to a nearby convenience store to pick up a gallon. I hugged Junior "goodnight," kissed my wife goodbye and hopped into the car for that short mile ride.

As I pulled into a parking space, a car (the only other vehicle in sight) caught my attention. I unbuckled my seatbelt, but I didn't hop out as I normally would. I found myself watching a young lady in the car next to mine. She was staring straight ahead with a blank look

on her face, the rumble of bass and a pounding country beat forcing its way out of the late-model Oldsmobuick.

Her fingers still clutched the steering wheel, occasionally tapping along to the beat. It appeared she was waiting for someone or something, but I didn't see anybody else in the store. It suddenly occurred to me that she was doing all she could to draw strength, somehow, from the song.

Finally, I stepped out of the car and walked toward the well-lit entrance. I glanced back at the girl, trying hard to be nonchalant. She still stared straight ahead, but now the blank look had melted to one of pain, even anguish. Feeling like I was hitting a brick wall, I choked back a lump before entering the store.

As I paid for my milk, my mind already had jumped to the situation outside and how to handle it. I received my change, grabbed my purchase and headed toward the exit with this heavily on my thoughts. I pushed open the door, and there she was, about to enter the store. I was startled. I stopped in my tracks, like we were old friends or something, and our eyes met for just a second.

She paid me no heed and, before my mouth could even form a simple "Hello," she had passed by. I went out and sat in the car, the image of her face in front of my mind, a face that showed signs of pain beyond her years. I was afraid to look at her as she soon left the store with a pack of cigarettes and carton of cookies.

It seemed as if the two of us had gone through something together when in reality it was just me. I did the only thing I could do. I put my car in gear, made my way home to the 'burbs and then, in the driveway, I wept. I contemplated the pain of another human being and, yes, I cried. With a fire's glow glistening through our front window, I stepped into the warmth of home. Junior, tucked away in bed, was asleep by now, and my wife sat reading quietly in front of the fireplace.

Later that night, as my wife and I lay in bed together, I shared with her what I had experienced at the convenience store. And she wept.

It may sound simple to say, but we've all been hurt. Sure, some have been hurt worse than others, but the principle is the same. We've got to shake it off, learn from what happened and move on before bitterness eats us inside out.

After all, life's too precious to live from one country song to another.

ALI AND ME

Not long ago I took my family with me on a business trip to Dallas, Texas. It was a whirlwind tour of two days of meetings and one fun-filled night with the family, and all went well. Upon returning from Dallas, our flight departed on time and arrived a little early in Chicago.

However, just as we were about to enter the line for our commuter flight home, the "Delayed" sign was posted next to our flight number. Shoot! The place was packed— people everywhere, some even sitting on the floor. After finding my wife and daughter a seat, I squeezed in just a row away.

Grumbling, laughing and chitchat filled this stuffy, stale-aired room and I, a little tired and irritable, somehow spotted a glimmer of hope. The lady next to me, reminiscent of my grandmother, pulled out a bag of homemade cookies (no frosting . . . hey, can't have everything) and began passing them out. Most folks were too polite or something to accept. I, on the other hand, held out both hands with glee.

After polishing off my fourth cookie, I began feeling comfortable in my surroundings and started to settle in. Just then I heard my wife's excited voice, in a stage whisper, pierce through the noisy crowd: "Troy, come here quick. Look!"

Lori doesn't have that note of urgency in her voice very often. In a split second I had jumped some fine luggage and dodged a pair of lovers and a sleeper only to find myself standing next to my wife.

Again she said, "Look!" So I looked . . . and looked again, and finally I saw: Muhammad Ali, the former three-time heavyweight boxing champion of the world, had entered our terminal. A hush fell over the entire place as he came in. He walked haltingly until his profile was but 10 feet from me. Suddenly he stopped, laboriously rotated his body to the left and looked directly into my eyes.

I glanced around quickly to make sure he was looking at me. There was no mistake. I was the only one

standing near. Like a scene from a movie, we were face-to-face, while everyone around us watched in wonder.

Finally, Ali cracked a huge grin—still looking into my eyes. He held it for a while and then he did it: gave me the quick one-two punch. He seemed to wait for a response. So I grinned and gave him a quick one-two back. Then he slowly turned . . . and walked away.

The crowd continued to watch to see if anything else would happen, but that was it. Ali soon disappeared into a throng of airport personnel.

The next several days I thought about this little encounter. What was it about this man that even now (old and feeble, suffering from Parkinson's disease) he reduces an airport terminal full of people to awe-inspired silence?

Confidence. At one time the world was his. Muhammad Ali had told us that he was "the greatest," and before long the world said the same. He even composed poems about his greatness. Goofy? Maybe, but he believed, and it came to pass.

Anything great that has ever been accomplished on this earth has been by men and women who dared to believe that they had something special to offer. And sure, not many can influence the entire world like Ali did, but we can all have an impact on our families, our friends and our communities for good—if we dare. There's so much potential in all of us awaiting that spark of confidence to ignite the fire of faith and greatness.

In the words of Ali and me: "Float like a butterfly, sting like a bee; dig down deep, and be who you're meant to be."

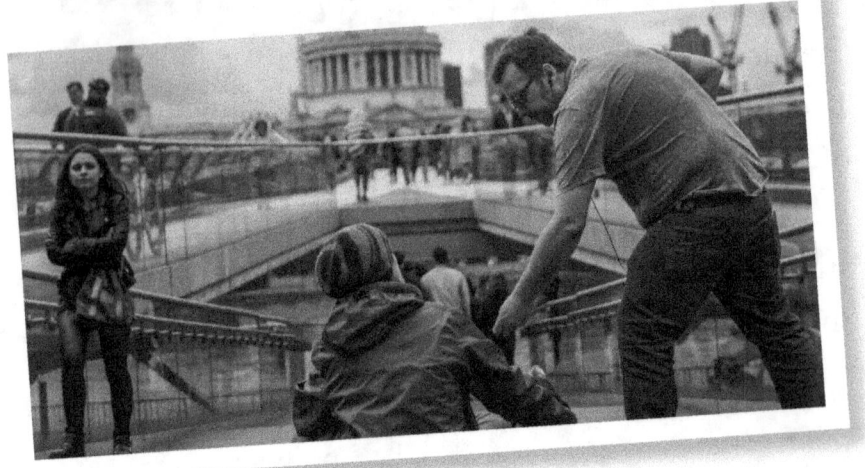

TANNEN: A SINGER, A WALLFLOWER, A SERVANT

Tannen is my little brother. We used to call him "Peanut" since he was born eight years after me. He seemed to be little and besides, he just looked like a peanut.

Tannen the person, though, couldn't be so easily classified. He loved to sing, and he loved to run from our Mother after she undressed him for his bath. I never forgot the afternoon my friend and I rolled into the driveway from a baseball game and there was Tannen on the front porch, not a stitch of clothes on his little body, singing at the top of his lungs. We couldn't understand a thing he was singing, but we knew he was happy.

As Tannen grew a little older, he began to find the joys of clothing and playing the part of several characters from the adult world he knew little about. His impersonations were uncanny. From ages four to seven, Tannen had several people down — their walk, their talk, their little idiosyncrasies like the tilt of a head or the curling of the fingers.

One of his first impersonations was of our preacher, Pastor Kern. Tannen would pull on his little sport coat, set up in a chair in the middle of the living room as his podium and start preachin'. You couldn't understand a word he said, but you didn't have to. He would fluctuate his voice to form shouts and dramatic pauses just like a pastor. Sometimes he would even pound the pulpit with passion.

Another favorite of Tannen's was a high school kid named Doug Wogoman. Tannen had seen him play a few times on the local basketball team. Doug would roll his shoulders forward when he ran, then receive a pass and take an unorthodox shot. Tannen would pick up on those nuances, as well as every detail of his game. He colored Doug's number and logo on his T-shirts. He would play ball in our living room in the same rhythm as Doug, which was amazing because most who

had watched that young man play never noticed his unique movements. Not only did Tannen notice, but he embraced them, then acted them out for all to see.

Inside this wildly creative kid was a quiet nature that few understood — even me at the time. I remember giving him my old minibike after I had moved onto a bigger one. I drove him around for a while and told him to hop on and take it for a spin. He was only 10, and he really didn't want to. However, I persisted, and he took off. He pulled the throttle all the way back and raced quickly down the trail behind the barn.

With mouth and eyes wide open, he headed straight for the railroad ditch. Fortunately, he grazed a tree branch, which landed him on the ground as he headed off the trail, flipping the bike over several times before they got to the ditch. He would've been fine, but the brake caught him on the leg, and he had to have five stitches. No more minibike rides for Tannen.

Similar things happened as he tried to jump into the world of school and relationships. Good friends were few and far between. His creative nature was pushed aside as his quieter nature took over and that quality tended to be misunderstood or simply abused. Regretfully, I too was guilty as I didn't bother taking the time to relate to the kid brother I hardly knew.

As Tannen bounced from grade to grade, he went largely unnoticed. Nobody seemed to have the time to receive what he had to give. And just as he had covered himself with various coats of creativity years before, he graduated from high school wearing a cloak of rejection.

But no need to worry about Tannen. After studying for a few years, he felt the call to those who need him most. This gentle wallflower is now working with homeless, drug-addicted, and down-trodden people in downtown New York City and someday hopes to serve overseas.

My hope is not just for my brother; he's finding his way. But what of the little ones who haven't and won't? The call is to all of us—parents, teachers, friends and family—to make room in our hearts for the sensitive souls.

WITH TODD, IT WAS A LITTLE ODD

As the proverb goes, "A friend is for all time, but a brother is born for adversity." I wish I had understood that as a child; it could have saved me some grief.

My brother is two years older than I, and seldom did we agree on anything. In our case, it wasn't so much adversity as it was simply very different approaches to life. For example, my Mother used to describe us this way: "If I would instruct the boys not to do something, Troy (that's me) would argue seven weeks from Sunday why he should be able to do it, while Todd would agree with me, then sneak off and do it anyway."

I harbor no bitterness toward my brother just because I was suspected and caught more in mischief than he. Our relational issues went deeper, and usually the conflict involved sports. Our Dad was a high school coach of several interscholastic sports, and Todd and I were both good athletes.

But no matter how well I did, Todd was older and in most sports just plain better. This was hard to take at times. If we played one-on-one basketball, you can bet that it ended with two boys rolling around on the court or the nearby grass trying to punch each other. For several years, fighting was something in which I could match him. I still remember the day that ended all fighting between us. I was 13 years old, and he was 15. We were playing basketball when a conflict flared. He quickly grabbed me and slung me to the floor like a sack of potatoes, and I knew that no matter how intense I was, fighting was no longer an option. Todd had suddenly hit his growth spurt.

From that point on, there was very little conflict — and very little relationship either. But there were still some things I admired about him. Todd had a style all his own. By the time he was a junior in high school, he was already considered one of the top basketball players in the area. He seemed to take it in stride, and nothing

seemed to be a big deal on or off the court. He was cool. And people liked him — well, except maybe the opposing team's crowd.

I'll never forget what Todd did at the end of a high school basketball game. This was Indiana where towns live and die by their basketball team. We were playing at home against another local rival. The gym was packed, and the game close. Finally, our team pulled away to a comfortable 4- or 5-point lead with just two seconds left in the game. My brother was taking the ball out of bounds beneath the opposing team's basket.

Despite their circumstances, the other team had not given up. An opposing player was jumping up and down, hounding Todd as he tried to pass the ball in to end the game. As the guy kept jumping and hand waving, Todd got a funny look on his face, then simply handed the kid the ball.

To say the least, he was perplexed by the sudden turn of events, but the kid managed to put the ball in the basket as the final horn sounded. The opposing team's crowd and coaches released an immediate roar of disapproval of my brother's "goodwill" gesture, as he would later call it.

The crowd quickly turned into a mob as my brother shrugged it off with his usual air of "I don't care." Our coach wisely ushered Todd into the locker room, then went back to try to appease the irate fans. Although Todd survived the misadventure, I recall another episode even more dangerous than angering a crowd of basketball fans. He angered Dad.

We were on our way to Florida for our family's annual Christmas trip. Todd was a junior in college and, I was a freshman. It would be our last trip together as an immediate family. Todd and I were in the back seat eating and drinking. I had a soda, and Todd sat sipping orange juice out of a glass bottle. While flying along the interstate, Todd rolled down his window and tossed the empty bottle up and back onto the highway.

I was shocked as I quickly turned and watched the bottle explode on the interstate pavement. Our Dad, who was driving, just happened to glance back and witness the entire event as well. It seemed to take a few seconds for him to comprehend what his eldest son had just done.

Next thing I knew, the car begins to swerve until we jolted to a disoriented halt at the side of the road. All the while, Dad was barking a chorus of "What kind of bonehead play was that? Don't you realize there are people on the highway and…?"

At one point Dad reached his right arm back toward Todd. That's the closest I ever came to being the oldest child. I think what made Dad so mad was Todd's response, which was one of innocence and perplexity, like "What's the big deal?" Knowing my brother, in his mind it was as if he were at a party and he simply disposed of an unwanted napkin.

We still take trips to Florida together, now with our families gathered 'round. Thankfully as my family and I follow his Ford Expedition full of kids down the highway, no stray bottles have erupted from his vehicle. And I can truly say that the "adversity" between Todd and me is gone.

Time, however, doesn't heal all wounds. Relationships must be pursued, which usually involves some sort of risk. But the payoff can be huge. Now instead of my mind replaying endless episodes of anger and regret, it's the occasional "get together" with stories and laughter 'round our dinner table following an evening meal, his children and mine enjoying the exaggerated childhood tales of two brothers who have learned to live and forgive. And sometimes even forget.

I guess everyone has a fire inside. And what could be banked coals of burning bitterness can also be a loving light that warms the bones at night, causing those who know forgiveness to say, "Life is good." Amen.

ABOUT THE AUTHOR

Troy Kidder is president of Kidder Media—a public relations/marketing firm specializing in print publications and digital media for schools and communities with a readership of millions per year and growing rapidly around the country. He is a pioneer in the industry of communications, public relations and marketing for schools, serving them for 25 years. Kidder has also done training for schools, businesses and even some Fortune 500 companies in the areas of Teamwork, Character, Bullying/Harassment and Creative Thinking. He also owns Kidder Crisis Communications which specializes in crisis prevention, crisis communications and crisis management.

A former high school English teacher, Kidder has written and published books including this book of stories, *LA4 Curriculum of Honor* for middle school students and the *LA4 Marketplace* for professional adults. He is also an entrepreneur, recording artist and outstanding public speaker. Kidder's family includes his wife, their married daughter, and two little girls. They make their home in Nashville, TN.

For more information about Troy's companies and materials, please see these links:
   www.kiddermedia.com
   www.kiddercrisiscommunications.com
   www.la4curriculum.com
   www.la4marketplace.com
   www.purebluecreative.com

www.ingramcontent.com/pod-product-compliance
Lightning Source LLC
Chambersburg PA
CBHW071159070526
44584CB00019B/2859